Oedipus Rex

By Sophocles

PRESTWICK HOUSE
LITERARY TOUCHSTONE CLASSICS™
P.O. Box 658 • Clayton, Delaware 19938

SENIOR EDITOR: Paul Moliken

EDITOR: Elizabeth Osborne

TRANSLATOR: J. E. Thomas

COVER DESIGN: Wendy Smith

PRODUCTION: Jerry Clark

PRESTWICK HOUSE
LITERARY TOUCHSTONE CLASSIC

P.O. BOX 658 • CLAYTON, DELAWARE 19938
TEL: 1.800.932.4593
FAX: 1.888.718.9333
WEB: www.prestwickhouse.com

Prestwick House Teaching Units™, *Activity Packs*™, *and Response Journals*™ *are the perfect complement for these editions. To purchase teaching resources for this book, visit www.prestwickhouse.com/material*

ISBN: 978-1-58049-593-6

Performance Note

Professionals and amateurs, please note that *Oedipus Rex*, translated by J. E. Thomas, is fully protected under the copyright laws of the United States and all countries within the copyright union. Performance rights are hereby granted for non-profit educational purpose. Performance rights for any for-profit purposes are reserved by the publisher. All inquiries related to obtaining performance rights and royalty rates should be directed to Jerry Clark, Prestwick House, Inc. P.O. Box 658 Clayton, DE 19938.

CONTENTS

NOTES

The *Oedipus Rex*, without argument one of the greatest plays ever written in any language, is also one of the most complex. Scholars have spent millennia debating Sophocles' intentions and how he achieved such a powerful effect. At the root of the play's popularity lies its humanity: All human beings search for themselves during life, and we all want to know who we really are. Through science, religion, and art, we try to discover who we are as a species—what it means to be human. This is precisely the search undertaken by Oedipus, and his quest to understand himself and its horrifying consequences resonate deeply inside all of us. The play communicates to us even though we are separated from it by time and language.

In preparing this translation from the Greek, I have used the Oxford text of Lloyd-Jones and Wilson. I have also availed myself of the excellent commentaries by Jebb and Kammerbeek. The manuscripts for the *Oedipus Rex*, although generally coherent, do contain several gaps and troublesome passages. In some cases, I have used an alternate reading to that of Lloyd-Jones and Wilson; in these instances, I generally follow the manuscript reading over the emendation and have rarely deviated without the authority of one of the commentators.

J. E. Thomas, Translator
Providence, R.I.

READING POINTERS

Reading Pointers for Sharper Insights

As you read *Oedipus Rex*, be aware of the following:

1. the role of dramatic irony in the play (the audience knows information, specifically about Oedipus' past, that the characters on stage do not).

2. the emergence of the following themes, concepts, and questions:
   - sin and retribution
   - divine justice: Do people deserve what happens to them, and do the gods allow it?
   - What characteristics make a good ruler?
   - The search for one's own identity is universal.
   - Complete control of one's own fate is not possible.
   - In life, suffering is inevitable, but wisdom can be gained through it.
   - There exists a need to search for truth.
   - What is the value of human intellect?

3. the conventions of Greek drama:
   - the use of masks with wigs attached
   - the Chorus, which would sing in verse and dance
   - multiple roles played by the same actor

DRAMATIS PERSONAE

Dramatis Personae

OEDIPUS, king of Thebes

the PRIEST of Zeus

CREON, Oedipus' brother-in-law

CHORUS of the old men of Thebes

TIRESIAS, blind prophet

JOCASTA, wife of Oedipus, sister of Creon, widow of Laius, the former king

MESSENGER from Corinth

SHEPHERD of Laius, the former king (in the manuscripts called the Servant)

SERVANT, from inside the house (in the manuscripts the Second Messenger or Messenger from the House)

OEDIPUS REX

[Scene: outside, in front of the palace of Oedipus. There is also a shrine to Apollo at which are seated many suppliants. Oedipus enters the stage from the palace.]

OEDIPUS: My children, new-sprung race of old Cadmus,[1]
    why do you sit at my shrines,[2] wearing garlands
    of the suppliants' olive?[3] All around
    the city is filled with the smell of incense,
5   all around filled with the sound of hymns and groans.
    These things I did not think it right to learn
    from messengers, and so I have come here myself,
    who am called Oedipus and known to all.
    But you, old man, tell me, since it is fitting
10   for you to speak on their behalf, why you
    sit out here, afraid of something or wanting it?
    So I would be willing to help you
    in any way, for he would be hardhearted
    who did not pity such an assembly.

15 PRIEST: Oedipus, you who rule my land, you see
    how many of us sit here at your altars;
    some do not yet have the strength to fly far;

[1]*Cadmus was the founder of Thebes; see* Thebes

[2]*shrines at his home, the palace, not shrines to him*

[3]*someone who makes requests from a position of powerlessness; see* Suppliant

others are heavy with age. I am the priest
of Zeus, and these[4] were chosen from the young men.

20 There is another group wreathed as suppliants
sitting in the marketplace[5] and another
at the double-gated temple of Athena[6]
and at the smoke-filled oracle of Ismenus.[7]
For the city, as you yourself can see,

25 is badly shaken already and from the waves
can no longer lift her head above this
bloody tossing; there is death in the fruitful buds
from the earth and in the pasturing herds,
and even in the childless births of women.[8]

30 Falling upon us, the fire-bringing god,[9]
most hateful disease, drives the city,
and by him the house of Cadmus is drained,
and dark Hades grows rich[10] with groans and wails.
Now, I do not hold you equal to the gods,

35 nor do these children who sit at your hearth,
but we judge you the first of men both
in the ordinary chances of life
and in the contingencies of the divine.[11]
It was you who came and released Cadmus' town

40 from the tribute we paid to the cruel songstress,[12]
and these things you did knowing nothing from us,
nor instructed at all, but with help from god
you spoke and knew how to set our lives straight.
And now, Oedipus, greatest in the eyes of all,

45 we who are here as your suppliants beseech you
to find some defense for us, as you may have heard
the voice of one of the gods or have learned
something from a man—for I think that the ideas
of experienced men most often succeed.

50 Come, o best of mortals, and save our city;
come, but be careful, since now this land
calls you her savior for your former zeal,
and let us never recall of your reign
that we first stood straight, but stumbled later.

55 Rather, then, restore this city to safety.

For at that time you gave us great fortune,
be now equal to what you were then.
Since, if indeed you would rule this land,
just as you do now, it is far better
60　　to rule over men than a wasteland;
nothing matters, neither tower nor ship,
if it is empty of men to dwell within it.

OEDIPUS:　My poor children, what you desire is
known and not unknown to me, for I see well
65　　that everyone is sick, and being sick,
still, not one of you is as sick as I am.
For your pain comes upon the individual,
one by one, to each man alone and no other,
but my soul groans for the city, for me and you
70　　together. Hence, you do not wake me from sleep,
but know that I have been weeping much
and wandering many roads of the mind.[13]
And that which my inquiry found our only cure
I have done, for I have sent Creon,
75　　son of Menoeceus, my own brother-in-law,
to Apollo's home at Pytho,[14] so that he may
learn what I should do or say to save this city.
And already enough time has passed that
I wonder what he is doing, for he has stayed
80　　beyond the proper time. But whenever he comes,
I would surely be an evil man not to do
whatever the god reveals.

PRIEST:　Wonderful news! Both what you have said,
and what these have just pointed out to me:
85　　Creon is approaching![15]

OEDIPUS:　Lord Apollo, if only he might come with
redeeming fortune as bright as shine his eyes!

PRIEST:　It seems he brings good news, for otherwise
he would not come crowned with berry-laden laurel.[16]

[13]*Sophocles emphasizes Oedipus' intellectual search. Oedipus' commitment to thought and humanist belief in human intelligence both characterize and doom him.*

[14]*Delphi, the most famous oracle in the Greco-Roman world*

[15]*Since Greek theaters are outdoors, and the stage entrances long and open, the audience would also be able to see Creon coming.*

[16]*The laurel was the tree of Apollo.*

90 OEDIPUS: We shall know soon, for he is close enough to hear.
       Lord, kinsman of my wife, child of Menoeceus,
       what reply do you bring us from the god?

[Enter Creon from offstage.]

CREON: A good one, for I say that even misfortunes,
       if somehow put right, bring only good luck.

95 OEDIPUS: What sort of reply is this? For what you say
       gives me neither confidence nor fear.

CREON: If you wish these people nearby to hear,
       I am ready to speak, or should we go inside?

OEDIPUS: Speak to everyone, for I consider their pain
100   more important even than that of my own soul.[17]

CREON: I shall say all I heard from the god.
       Phoebus clearly ordered us, my lord,
          to drive out the pollution being fostered
       in this very land, not to nurture it unhealed.[18]

105 OEDIPUS: With what cleansing and for what type of disaster?

CREON: By driving a man into exile,
       or undoing murder with murder again,
          since this blood shakes our city like a storm.

OEDIPUS: And who is the man whose fate he decrees?

110 CREON: My lord, once Laius was our leader in this land,
       before you came to govern this city.

OEDIPUS: So I have heard, though I never saw him.

CREON: He died, and the god now orders us clearly
       to take violent vengeance on the murderers.

[17]*It is important that Sophocles characterizes Oedipus as a good king. He feels concern for his people and rules justly.*

[18]*The Greeks believed that, when a murder was committed, the murderer, the place of the crime, and any place that harbored the killer were polluted, that is, outside the favor of the gods; see* Pollution

115 OEDIPUS: Where on earth are they? Where will be found
    this indistinct track of ancient guilt?[19]

CREON: In this very land, he said. What is sought
    can be captured, but what is ignored escapes.

OEDIPUS: Did Laius meet his bloody fate in his home
120   or estate or in some other land?

CREON: He left home to consult an oracle, he said,
    and never returned again, once he had set out.

OEDIPUS: Did no messenger or fellow traveler see,
    whom we might use to find something out?

125 CREON: No, they died, except one, who, fleeing in fear
    of those he saw, had nothing to say but one thing.

OEDIPUS: What? For one thing could lead us to learn many,
    if from hope might come a small beginning.

CREON: He said that bandits fell upon them and killed him,
130   not with one man's strength, but the hands of many.

OEDIPUS: How did a bandit come to dare so much,
    unless he acted with money from here?[20]

CREON: This was suspected. But with Laius fallen,
    we had no helper in our troubles.

135 OEDIPUS: What kind of trouble, when your kingship had
    fallen thus, made you see to this so poorly?

CREON: The riddle-singing Sphinx compelled us to look
    at what lay at hand, forgetting things unseen.

OEDIPUS: Then I shall reveal these things anew,
140   for justly did Phoebus, and justly did you
    assign me this case on behalf of the dead,

[19]*Some people have read the* Oedipus Rex *as a kind of detective story. It is, of course, much more than that, but we do see Oedipus pursuing clues and reasoning through arguments. Sophocles emphasizes this intellectual process more than in other plays.*

[20]*Oedipus immediately suspects a treasonous conspiracy in Thebes to assassinate the king.*

so that you will rightly see me as an ally,
avenging both this land and the god together.[21]
For not on behalf of more distant friends,
145 but as if from myself I shall dispel the stain.[22]
For whoever he was who killed that man
would as soon kill me with that same violent hand.
Helping that one, therefore, I am helping myself.
But you, my children, as soon as you can, rise
150 from these seats, stopping these suppliant wails.
Someone, muster here the people of Cadmus,
as I will leave nothing undone. For with God's help
we shall see whether we are saved or lost.

PRIEST: Let us stand up, my children; those things for which
155 we came here this man himself has promised.
But may Phoebus who sent these prophecies
come at once as savior and stayer[23] of disease!

                                    [Exeunt omnes.]
                    [The Chorus marches into the orchestra.[24]]

CHORUS: Str 1[25]
     O sweetly worded voice of Zeus, who are you
     who come from all-gold Pytho to glorious Thebes?[26]
160 My frightened mind shakes in fear, quivering,
     o healing Delian Paean,[27]
     in awe before you. What is it you will achieve for me,
     something new or something known and coming back
                         again?
     Tell me, o child of golden Hope,
165 immortal Utterance.

                                                 Ant 1
     First I call on you, daughter of Zeus, immortal Athena,
     and your earth-protecting sister, Artemis,
     who sit, famous, on your throne in the marketplace;[28]
     and Phoebus the farshooter
170 I call: my threefold protection from death, shine forth on me.
     If ever when madness was set upon the city,
     you sent away our burning scourge,
     come also now.

                                                          Str 2

Alas! for I bear countless woes;
175   disease falls upon my entire crew,
and no mind's weapon can protect me,
for the fruit of our famous land does not grow,
nor do our women emerge from their
mournful labors with offspring.
180   One upon another you might see each soul,
like a well-winged bird, surer than irresistible fire,
setting out for the promontory of the western god.[29]

                                                          Ant 2

Unable to count their number,
the city is destroyed, and, unpitied,
185   their generations lie upon the ground,
spreading death, finding no mourners.
While brides and white-haired mothers come together
and groan as suppliants over their mournful labors,
the hymn for healing and the lament ring loud together.
190   Because of these, o golden daughter of Zeus,
send bright-eyed Strength.

                                                          Str 3

Furious Ares,[30] now without bronze shields,[31]
yet still surrounded by cries, confronts me and burns me;
let him, in hurried running, turn his back
195   on our fatherland, either borne by a wind
into the great chamber of Amphitrite[32]
or rushing to the inhospitable Thracian wave.[33]
For, if night ever leaves something undone,
day comes along to complete it.
200   This one, o reverend lightning-bearer,
father Zeus, make him perish with your thunderbolt.

                                                          Ant 3

And you, lord of light,[34] from your golden bow
I would have your unconquered arrows fly
as a guard set in front of me before my enemy,
205   and those of shining, fire-bringing Artemis,
with which she darts across the hills of Lycia.
And I call upon the one with the golden headband,
eponym of this land,[35] wine-faced Bacchus,

[29]*the region of sunset, the realm of Death*

[30]*the god of war, particularly its irrational destruction. Here he is invoked as a figure of rampant devastation in general, the plague specifically.*

[31]*The Chorus pray to fight fire with fire, i.e., to fight the destructive fire of Ares and the plague with the beneficial fires of Zeus's thunderbolt, of Apollo's and Artemis' flashing arrows, and of Dionysus' torches.*

[32]*an ocean goddess*

[33]*the Atlantic Ocean and the Black Sea, considered by the Greeks the edges of the world.*

[34]*Apollo*

[35]*Dionysus (or Bacchus) was the son of a Theban princess, so Thebes is sometimes called "Bacchic."*

[36]Maenads were nymphs who followed Dionysus everywhere he went.

[37]i.e., Ares

[38]Since he replies to the Chorus' prayers, Oedipus may have entered during the latter part of their song. His speech marks the return to normal dialogue from the choral ode.

[39]These lines in the manuscript are very corrupt, an unfortunately common occurrence in the surviving literature from ancient Greece. The lines given reflect what seems to be the sense.

[40]Oedipus' words are binding on all Thebans, so he has to make allowances for the possibility that a foreigner killed Laius. Here he refers to two groups: Thebans and everyone else.

[41]Oedipus forbids the killer to take part in any religious rites; the gods would be offended by the presence of a polluted man, and so the sacrifice would be in vain.

hailed companion of the Maenads' throng,[36]

210   to approach with a torch of shining pine,

against this god[37] dishonored by the gods.

[Enter Oedipus from the palace.[38]]

OEDIPUS: You seek, and what you seek, if you are willing
     to listen to my words and help in this sickness,
     you may take as help and relief from your troubles.
215   Although a stranger to both report and victim,
     I shall announce these things, for I would not be far
     in tracking it, if I did not have some clue.
     But now, since only later did I become
     a citizen among citizens, I decree
220   the following to the people of Cadmus:
     whoever among you knows at whose hands
     Laius son of Labdacus was destroyed,
     I order this man to tell it all to me.
     And if the culprit fears this accusation,[39]
225   he should lose his fear and come forward,
     for he will suffer nothing worse than safe exile
     from this land. But if someone knows that another
     or one from some other land is the murderer,[40]
     let him not be silent! For I myself
230   shall complete his reward, and he will have
     my favor. But if you are silent again,
     and someone out of fear pushes away
     responsibility from himself or a friend,
     then you must hear from me what I intend to do.
235   I ban this man, whoever he is, from all land
     over which I hold power and the throne.
     I decree that no one shall receive him
     or speak to him, nor make him partner
     in prayers to the gods or sacrifices,
240   nor allow to him holy water;
     but instead that everyone must expel him
     from their homes,[41] as this man is the source
     of our pollution, as the oracle
     of Pytho has just revealed to me.

245   And so I myself am become an ally
        both to the god and the man who died.
        And I curse the doer, whether he worked alone
        or evaded us with accomplices,
        that he wear out his unlucky life
250   as badly as he himself is bad.
        And I pray, if he should be known to me
        and share in my hearth among my family,
        that I suffer all that I called upon these.[42]
        All these things I charge you to complete,
255   on my behalf and on the god's, and for this land,
        wasted away, fruitless and godless.
        But even if this problem were not put
        before us by god, you should not suffer
        this unclean thing, since the man lost was
260   both very noble and your king, so see this through.
        Now, since I am ruler and hold this kingdom
        that he held before—holding also the bed
        and wife we have both sown; and children
        of the same mother would have been born to us,
265   had his line not been ill-fated—since chance
        has driven me into that one's powers,
        therefore I shall fight for him in this matter,
        as if for my own father, and I shall try
        everything, seeking to find the one who
270   committed the murder, for Labdacus' son,
        son of Polydorus, and before him
        Cadmus and Agenor, kings of old.
        I pray god that to those who do not do these things
        no crop may spring up from the ground, nor children
275   from their wives, but they be destroyed in suffering
        more hateful than that which holds us now.
        But to you other people of Cadmus,
        to however many approve what I say,
        may Justice and all the gods stay with you
280   always as your ally.

        CHORUS:[43] Just as you adjured me under a curse, my lord,
        so shall I speak. For neither did I kill

[42] A crucial moment in the play. The audience would know that Oedipus, himself the murderer, becomes the agent of his own destruction through his own curse.

[43] The dialogue lines designated "Chorus" were probably spoken by a single "Chorus-leader," hence the singular pronouns. He speaks, however, for the Chorus as a whole, who, in turn, represent the citizen body of Thebes.

nor am I able to show the killer.
But it is the task of the one who sent it,
285   Phoebus, to say whoever has done this thing.

OEDIPUS: You have spoken justly, but no man can
compel the gods when they are unwilling.

CHORUS: I would say things secondary to this,
but things which, I think, ought to be said.

290 OEDIPUS: And if there are matters tertiary to it,
do not fail to say them also.

CHORUS: I know that my lord Tiresias most always
sees the same as my lord Apollo; from him one
investigating this might learn the wisest things.

295 OEDIPUS: But this has not been neglected! No,
even this I have done, for I sent two guides
after Creon mentioned him, and it is surprising
only that he is not already here.

CHORUS: There are still other reports, though mute and old...

300 OEDIPUS: What's this? I will investigate any story.

CHORUS: It is said he died at the hands of bandits.

OEDIPUS: So I have heard, but no one sees the one who saw.

CHORUS: But if he has any fear at all, hearing
such curses as yours he will not remain here.

305 OEDIPUS: But to a man who does not shrink from doing
the thing, a word will not be frightening.

CHORUS: But the one to accuse him is here, for
already those men lead hither the godlike
seer, in whom alone of men lives the truth.

[Enter Tiresias, led by guides.]

310 OEDIPUS: O Tiresias, who grasps all things,
     both what can be learned and what is unspeakable,
     both of heaven and treading the earth,
     even if you cannot see, you still understand
     what sickness plagues our city, and we find, lord,
315   you alone are our savior and defender.
     For Phoebus, if you have not heard this also
     from the messengers, in response to our question
     said relief from this sickness would only come
     if we should discover and punish well
320   the murderers of Laius or send them forth
     as fugitives from this land. Therefore,
     grudging nothing from the speech of birds[44]
     or something known from another sort
     of divination, save yourself and the city,
325   and save me, and ward off all the pollution[45]
     from the dead man. We are in your hands,
     and to help a man from troubles when you have
     the power is the sweetest of labors.

TIRESIAS: Alas, alas! How terrible to know
330   when it does not help the knower; for knowing this
     well I let it slip—I should not have come here.

OEDIPUS: What's this? How dispiritedly you have come!

TIRESIAS: Send me home, for you will bear your lot easily
     and I mine, if you will yield to me.

335 OEDIPUS: You speak neither clearly nor helpfully
     to this city, which raised you, if you guard your thoughts.

TIRESIAS: For I see that your words come at the wrong time,
     and since I would not suffer the same thing...

OEDIPUS: No, by the gods, don't hold back what you know, when
340   all of us as suppliants bow down before you.[46]

[44] Observing the flight of birds was an important aspect of Greek prophecy, as their motions were thought to indicate the gods' will.

[45] or miasma; see note 18

[46] The Greeks bowed down only before gods, so this is a very strong gesture of Tiresias' special status.

TIRESIAS: None of you understand, but I shall never
reveal my own troubles, and so I shall not say yours.

OEDIPUS: What are you saying? You will not explain
what you understand, but rather intend
345   to betray us and destroy the city.

TIRESIAS: I cause no pain for you or myself. Why do you
vainly seek this? For you can learn nothing from me.

OEDIPUS: You worst of wicked men! You would anger
a stone! Will you reveal nothing, but instead
350   show yourself unmovable and impractical?

TIRESIAS: You have found fault with my anger, but your own,
living within you, you did not see, but blamed me.

OEDIPUS: Who could hear such words and not grow angry,
words with which you dishonor the city?

355 TIRESIAS: It will end the same, though I hide it in silence.

OEDIPUS: Why not, then, tell me what will come anyway?

TIRESIAS: I should explain no further. At these things,
if you wish, rage as much as your heart is able.

OEDIPUS: Indeed, since I am so angry, I'll pass over none
360   of what I understand. Know that I think
you, too, had your hand in this deed and did it,
even though you did not kill with your own hands.
But if you could see, I would think the deed yours
            alone.[47]

TIRESIAS: Really? I say to you: Abide by that decree
365   you made earlier, and from this day address
neither these men here nor me, since you
are the unholy polluter of this land.

[47]Remember that
Oedipus has
doubted the bandit
story from the
beginning and
always suspected
a conspiracy in
Thebes.

OEDIPUS: Did you throw out this word so boldly?
And where do you think you will escape it?[48]

[48]*i.e., How can you escape the consequences of this accusation?*

370 TIRESIAS: I *have* escaped it, for I hold the potent truth.

OEDIPUS: Who told you to say this? It is no prophecy!

TIRESIAS: You did! For you forced me to speak unwillingly!

OEDIPUS: What do you mean? Speak again, that I may learn more.

TIRESIAS: Didn't you understand before? Or do you test me?

375 OEDIPUS: No, I don't know what you mean. Explain again.

TIRESIAS: I say that you slew the man whose slayer you seek.

OEDIPUS: You'll not rejoice to have said these evils twice.

TIRESIAS: Should I now say more, too, to anger you further?

OEDIPUS: Whatever you deem best; it will be said in vain.

380 TIRESIAS: I say that you secretly have lived most foully
with those who should be most dear, nor do you see
to what extent of evil you have come.

OEDIPUS: Do you really think you can say this unpunished?

TIRESIAS: If there is any strength in the truth.

385 OEDIPUS: There is, but not for you. You don't have this,
since you are blind in your ears and mind and eyes.

TIRESIAS: You are truly pathetic, hurling these insults,
which soon every man here will hurl at you.

OEDIPUS: You live in one single night, so that you can never
390 harm me or any other who sees the light.

TIRESIAS: No, for fate will not befall you at my doing;
        Apollo is enough, who works to see this done.

OEDIPUS: Did Creon invent all this, or someone else?

TIRESIAS: Creon is no burden on you, but you on yourself.

395 OEDIPUS: O wealth and power and skill reaching
        beyond skill, in a much-envied life
        how much resentment gathers up inside you,
        if for the sake of this realm, which the city put
        into my hands as a gift, not something sought,
400   the trusted Creon, my friend from the beginning,
        beguiles me and secretly desires to oust me,
        engaging this craftily-working wizard,
        this tricky beggar, who sees clearly only
        for profit, but is blind when it comes to skill.

405   So tell me, when are you the wise seer?
        How is it that, when the singing hound[49] was here,
        you never said how the citizens might be freed?
        Even though the riddle could not be solved by
        the first man who met it, but required prophecy.
410   But you did not come forth with this, knowing some clue
        from birds or gods; instead I came along,
        the idiot Oedipus! I stopped her,
        working from intellect, not learning from birds.
        The very man you're trying to overthrow,
415   thinking to stand beside Creon's throne.
        I think you both—you and the one who framed these
            things—
        will regret your urge to cleanse the land, but if you
        were not so old, you'd learn now what such words earn.

420 CHORUS: To us it seems that both this man's words
        and your own, Oedipus, were said in anger.
        But we must not dwell on such things. Only this:
        how best we may fulfill the gods' instructions.[50]

[49]The Sphinx was sent by Hera in anger at the Thebans to guard them closely; the monster is compared to a dog with its prey at bay.

[50]The Chorus pleads for a more civic-minded attitude from both men, especially Oedipus, but is ignored.

TIRESIAS: Even though you are a tyrant, I must at least
425   be granted an equal reply, for I, too,
      have the right to speech. For I am no slave to you,
      at all, but to Loxias,[51] so I will not be
      written off as Creon's client.[52] I will reply,
      since you reproach me as blind: You, even though you
430   see clearly, do not see the scope of your evil,
      nor where you live, nor with whom you dwell.
      Do you know your true descent? And secretly
      you are an enemy to your own kin,
      both under the earth and on it.[53] Striking you
435   from both sides the terrible hounds[54] of your mother's
      and father's curse will drive you from this land;
      though you see well enough now, then you will be blind.
      What place will not be harbor to your shouting?
      What Cithaeron will not echo back your cries,[55]
440   when you truly understand that wedding?
      You sailed home into it, no proper harbor
      after such good sailing before! Nor do you
      perceive the multitude of other evils,
      which will make you the equal of your children.
445   Go ahead—insult Creon and this mouth of mine,
      for of all mortals who will be destroyed
      root and branch, there is not one sadder than you.

OEDIPUS: Am I to tolerate hearing this from this man?
      No, to hell with him! No! Turn around quickly
450   and head back home, far away from here.

TIRESIAS: I would not have come here, if you had not called me.

OEDIPUS: I did not know what nonsense you would speak,
      or I would hardly have sent for you.

TIRESIAS: Men like myself are born, to your eyes, fools,
455   but to the parents who bore you we seem wise.

OEDIPUS: To whom? Wait! Who on earth are my parents?[56]

[51]another name for Apollo, one particularly associated with his role as a god of prophecy

[52]As a citizen, Tireseias does not need Creon to stand up for him, but can speak for himself. The metaphor is drawn from Athenian legal procedure.

[53]i.e., both to the dead Laius and the living Jocasta

[54]The Greek has "terror-footed curse," meaning the curse will track Oedipus relentlessly. This is a common image in Greek poetry for the Furies, frightening and ancient goddesses who pursue and drive mad those who have sinned against their own kin.

[55]the mountain on which Oedipus was abandoned; see Cithaeron

[56]As Oedipus reveals later, this question has long bothered him.

TIRESIAS: This very day will sire you and destroy you.

OEDIPUS: How riddling and foolish is all you say!

TIRESIAS: Then you of all people should understand it.[57]

460 OEDIPUS: With these same taunts you now hurl, you will
find me great.

TIRESIAS: This same stroke, however, has destroyed you.

OEDIPUS: But if I saved this city, that doesn't matter.

TIRESIAS: Then I will leave. You, boy, lead me home.

OEDIPUS: Yes, go! When you are here, you are in the way,
465   but rushing off you cannot pain us further.

TIRESIAS:[58] I will leave after I have said what I came to say,
not fearing your face, for you cannot destroy me.
I say to you: That man, whom you have long sought,
threatening him and naming as the murderer
470 of Laius, that man is here.
An immigrant in theory, soon he will be
revealed a native Theban, though he will not be
happy to learn it; for blind instead of seeing,
a beggar instead of rich he will travel
475 foreign earth, tapping it with his staff.
He will be revealed to live with his children
as brother and father both; and to his parents
he is both his wife's son and lord and his father's
fellow-sower and slayer. Go inside and
480 consider this. Should you find that I am lying,
you will prove I have no skill at prophecy.
                              [Exeunt omnes except Chorus]

CHORUS:[59]   *Str. 1*
Who was it the oracle-speaking
rock of Delphi[60] saw

---

[57]Allusions to the Sphinx and Oedipus' victory over her dominate the next few lines.

[58]Since ancient plays lack stage directions, we do not know if Oedipus remains on stage for this speech or reenters the palace.

[59]Since choral odes usually comment on all the action that has happened since the last ode, the Chorus deal with Oedipus' decree in the first strophe-antistrophe pair and then the confrontation with Tiresias in the second strophe-antistrophe pair.

[60]Apollo's oracle at Delphi was cradled in tall mountains, and the murder occurred at the crossroads leading to Delphi, so the Chorus are correct to call the rock of Delphi a literal witness to the murder—they do not do so merely because of Apollo's gift of prophetic sight.

committing the most unspeakable acts
485   with red hands?
Now, stronger than swift-footed horses,
he must deftly move his foot in flight.
For in arms against him leaps
the son of Zeus with fire and lightning
490   and, following after him,
the terrible, unerring Furies.

                                   Ant. 1

For, recently from snowy Parnassus
shone clearly the call
to track by every possible method
495   the unknown man.
For he wanders through the wild wood
and up to caves like a bull upon the rocks,[61]
miserable, with miserable foot, living alone,
seeking to escape the prophecies
500   of the prophetic navel of the world,[62]
yet they forever hover, living, around him.

                                   Str. 2

Therefore, terribly, terribly does
the wise bird-interpreter shake
me; I can neither approve nor deny,
505   but I am confused.
My heart hovers with expectation,
seeing neither here nor in the future.
For never have I learned
that any quarrel lay between
510   the Labdacids and the son of Polybus,[63]
neither before nor now,
which I could use as proof
or trust as touchstone[64]
to go against the public fame of Oedipus
515   as I seek to help the Labdacids
in the undiscovered murder.

                                   Ant. 2

But, though Zeus and Apollo know
the ways of mortals, among men,
there is no sure rule that a seer's opinion

[61] This passage is convoluted in the original Greek, and some scholars feel that the text is corrupt in this stanza.

[62] Apollo's oracle at Delphi, the most important place of prophecy in the Greek world and hence one of the few symbols of Greek cultural unity, was often called the Navel of the World; see Oracles

[63] The Chorus still believe Polybus, the King of Corinth and Oedipus' adoptive father, is, in fact, his real father.

[64] a hard stone used to test the purity of precious metals

520   counts more than mine,
       though a man may surpass wisdom
       with his own wisdom.
       But, no, until I see an account
       confirmed, never would I
525   agree when men are speaking slanders.
       For once the winged maiden
       came openly against him,
       and he was seen wise
       and found friendly to the city; therefore
530   by the judgment of my mind
       never will he merit suspicion.

       [Enter Creon from offstage.]

       CREON: Gentlemen of the city, I have learned that
          the tyrant Oedipus has spoken terrible
          words against me, so I am here, unable
535   to bear it. If in our present distress
          he thinks he has suffered at my hands,
          then I have no desire for long life
          if I must bear this reputation, for
          its damage affects no single part of my life,
540   rather the greatest part of it, if I am called
          base in my city, base even by my friends.

       CHORUS: But, while this censure did come, it came quickly
          and pushed out in anger, not from rational thoughts.

       CREON: Was it said that won over by advice
545   of mine the seer uttered false words?

       CHORUS: He said these things, but I do not know why.

       CREON: Did he make this accusation of me
          with eyes set straight and from his right mind?

       CHORUS: I don't know, for what rulers do, I do not see.[65]

[65] *The Chorus adopts a deliberately noncommittal position.*

[*Enter Oedipus from the palace.*]

550   OEDIPUS: You there, how did you come here? Or do you have
         so much daring that you approach my roof,
         although the patent murderer of this man[66]
         and the manifest thief of my kingdom?
         Come then, say, by the gods, did you think me a fool
555   or coward that you would weave these schemes?
         That I would not discover this deed of yours
         creeping forth in treachery or, when I learned,
         I would not defend myself? Isn't this venture
         of yours foolish, to hunt tyranny
560   without wealth or friends, a thing captured only
         with a mob and money?

      CREON: Do you know what you should do? Hear an answer in
         response to your speech, then learn and judge for yourself.

      OEDIPUS: You're a clever speaker, but I'm a bad student,
565   for I have found you hostile and troubling to me.

      CREON: Hear now this one thing that I came to say.

      OEDIPUS: 'This one thing' should not be that you are not false.

      CREON: If you think that stubbornness is of value
         apart from reason, you are a madman!

570   OEDIPUS: If you think a man who does his kinsman ill
         will not pay the price, you are a fool.

      CREON: I understand you think these things legitimate,
         but tell me what suffering you had at my hands.

      OEDIPUS: Did you or did you not persuade me that I must
575   send a man for the reverend seer?

      CREON: Even now I hold the same opinion.

[66]i.e., Oedipus

OEDIPUS: How long a time has passed since Laius...

CREON: Did what deed? I do not understand.

OEDIPUS: ...wanders invisible, conquered by death?

580 CREON: Many long years have been measured out since then.

OEDIPUS: Next, was this seer in business at that time?

CREON: Just as wise and revered as he is today.

OEDIPUS: Did he say anything about me at the time?

CREON: Never when I stood near and listened.

585 OEDIPUS: Did you not hold an inquiry for the killer?

CREON: We held one; how could we not? Yet we heard nothing.

OEDIPUS: How, then, did this wise man not tell you anything?

CREON: I don't know; I prefer to keep quiet
        in matters when I don't comprehend them.

590 OEDIPUS: There is one thing you could say with comprehension...

CREON: What is it? If I know, I will not deny it.

OEDIPUS: For whom, if he did not meet with you, did he say
        that the death of Laius was my work?

CREON: If he says that, then he himself knows, but I
595   would learn from you, as you now ask from me.

OEDIPUS: Learn away! For I will not be caught as slayer.

CREON: Well, then—are you still married to my sister?

OEDIPUS: There is no denial of your question.

CREON: Do you grant equal rule of this land to her?

600 OEDIPUS: All that she desires she has from me.

CREON: Am I not, then, the third, equal with you both?

OEDIPUS: Indeed, for it's here you are proved a bad friend.

CREON: Not if you would reckon with yourself as I do!
 Consider this first: Would anyone choose
605 to rule with fear rather than to sleep untrembling,
 if he could have the same power? And so I
 myself was not born preferring to be tyrant
 rather than do a tyrant's acts, nor was
 any other who has good sense. For now I have
610 everything from you without fear; but if I
 myself were ruler, I'd do much against my will.
 How then could tyranny be sweeter to me
 than trouble-free rule and sovereignty?[67]
 In no way will you find me so deceived
615 that I require fair things that hold no profit.
 Now I can be with anyone; all salute me.
 Now those wanting something from you call on me;
 I am their whole path to success. How could I
 exchange this life for the other? An evil mind
620 could not reason fairly. But I am no lover
 of such schemes,[68] anyway, nor would I ever
 support it even if another did the deed.
 And this will be the proof of it: go to Pytho
 and learn the oracles, if I have
625 reported them correctly. Then, if you catch me
 plotting something with the seer, don't kill me
 with one vote, but with two, mine and yours.
 But, don't blame me just like that, with mere suspicion.
 For it is not just either to randomly
630 consider wicked men good or the good wicked.
 I think that casting off a good friend is equal

[67]*The idea that the tyrant's life is bad because he must be constantly vigilant and can never relax is common in Greek literature and philosophy.*

[68]*i.e., the imagined conspiracy with Tiresias to overthrow Oedipus*

even to throwing out one's own dear life.
In time, though, you will surely know these things, since
time alone shows that a man is just,
635   but you might learn he is bad in a single day.

CHORUS: He spoke as one should to a man worried he will
fall, my lord, for quick thinkers are not safe ones.

OEDIPUS: Whenever someone swiftly moves secret plots
against me, I must also counter-plot swiftly.
640   But if I wait in silence, these things will be
accomplished, not as his deeds, but my mistakes.

CREON: What do you want? To cast me from this land?

OEDIPUS: Hardly—I want you to die, not flee.

CREON:[60] You are the form of jealousy.

[60]The text at these
lines is very cor-
rupt; it is obvious
that some lines
have been lost.

645   OEDIPUS: You speak neither to concede nor to persuade?

CREON: For I see well that you do not understand.

OEDIPUS: I understand my own affairs well enough.

CREON: You must know mine equally well.

OEDIPUS: Not when they are false!

650   CREON: Do you understand nothing?

OEDIPUS: Yet, there must be rule.

CREON: Not if ruled badly!

OEDIPUS: O city, city!

CREON: The city is mine, too, not yours alone!

655 CHORUS: Stop, my lords! I see, at just the right moment,
Jocasta, coming from the house to you, with whom
you ought to settle this present quarrel.

[Enter Jocasta from the palace.]

JOCASTA: Why, unhappy men, do you stir up this
unwelcome revolution of the tongue? Aren't you
660   ashamed to stir private evils when the land is
so sick? Come inside, and you, Creon, return home;
don't make this foolish grief into something big.

CREON: Sister, this husband of yours, Oedipus, judges
terrible things for me, choosing two evils:
665   to forsake my fatherland or to die.

OEDIPUS: I concede this, for, my lady, I caught him
basely conspiring against me with evil craft.

CREON: May I live no more, but die accursed, if I have done
against you any of what you accuse me.[70]

670 JOCASTA: By the gods, Oedipus, believe this,
respecting this oath to the gods most of all,
then me and these who are here with you.

Str.

CHORUS:[71] Yield to these wishes and thoughts,
my lord, I pray.

675 OEDIPUS: What would you have me yield?

CHORUS: Respect a man who never before was foolish
and now is powerful from his oath.

OEDIPUS: Do you know what you seek?

CHORUS: I do.

680 OEDIPUS: Then tell me why.

[70]Oaths are serious business in Greek tragedy and Greek thought in general, so this is an extremely strong statement of innocence from Creon.

[71]Here begins the first kommos, a lyric song sung by the characters and Chorus together. Note how, while both Chorus and characters are very emotional, their concerns are different: The Chorus are, as always, concerned with the city's welfare, the individual characters with the problems of their family. There is some regular dialogue between the strophe and antistrophe, and the Chorus here do most of the singing.

CHORUS: Never should you cast out a friend who is
    bound with an oath,
  dishonored, with only the charge of obscure words.

OEDIPUS: Know well that when you seek this, you seek either
  my destruction or exile from this land.

685 CHORUS: No, by the foremost of all the gods,[72]
    the Sun! May I perish godless and friendless,
    the worst fate, if I have this in mind!
    But for me, the dying land eats away
    at my ill-starred heart, if this fight between you two
690   will join itself to our old problems.

OEDIPUS: Then let him go, since I must either die
  or be driven by force from this land, dishonored.
  For I pity your speech, since it is piteous,
  not his. He will be hated wherever he goes.

695 CREON: You are clearly hateful in yielding, and severe
   when you pass from anger. But personalities
   like yours are justly painful to themselves.

OEDIPUS: Will you not let me be and go away?

CREON: I'll go,
700 finding you ignorant, but just in their eyes.[73]
           [Exit Creon offstage.]

               Ant.

CHORUS: Lady, why do you hesitate
  to take this man inside the house?

JOCASTA: I would learn what has befallen.

CHORUS: Suspicion through unknown words
705 came, and even an unjust word can bite.

JOCASTA: From both of them?

[72] *i.e., by the god who is most evident to human sight, the all-seeing Sun*

[73] *i.e., Creon thinks the Chorus will see him as just.*

CHORUS: Yes.

JOCASTA: But, what was the cause?

CHORUS: It has done enough to me, enough when the land
710   already suffers so, that it should stay departed.

OEDIPUS: Do you see where you've gotten, despite your good
        intentions, trying to ease and blunt my anger?

CHORUS: My lord, I've said it not only once,
        but know that I am mad, helpless in rational thought,
715   if I forsake you,
        who, when my dear country was lost in troubles,
        set her upright again.
        But now, become once more our guide to better things![74]

[74]Here ends the kommos.

JOCASTA: By the gods, tell me also, my lord,
720   what problem puts you in so much anger!

OEDIPUS: Since I respect you, my wife, more than them, I shall
        speak of Creon and what he plots against me.

725 JOCASTA: Speak, if you will explain the quarrel clearly.

OEDIPUS: He said I was the murderer of Laius.

JOCASTA: Knowing this for himself, or learning from hearsay?

OEDIPUS: He sent that criminal seer, since regarding
        his own affairs, he keeps his tongue unstained.

730 JOCASTA: You now, free yourself from these matters;
        listen to me and learn why nothing mortal
        can show you anything of prophecy.[75]
        I shall tell a quick tale to prove my words.
        A prophecy came to Laius once—I won't say
735   from Apollo himself, but from his servants[76]—
        that death would come to him from his child,

[75]Jocasta does not answer Oedipus' charge against Creon, but moves to discredit Tiresias. While this speech is necessary for the drama of Oedipus' identity to progress, it is something of a non sequitur here.

[76]Note that Jocasta here does not doubt the credibility of all oracles; she trusts the god himself, but not his mortal agents.

whoever was born to him from me. But then,
just as the report is, some foreign brigands
slew him where the three wagon-roads meet.
740   Yet three days had not passed from the birth of my child,
when that man, binding his ankles together,
sent him in another's hands into the wild
of the mountain. And so Apollo brought about
neither that he slay his father nor that Laius
745   suffer the terrible thing he feared from his child.
Such things the speeches of seers predict,
you should ignore; for whatever the god
requires, he himself will easily reveal.

OEDIPUS: Hearing you just now, my lady, how
750   my soul wanders, how my mind shakes me!

JOCASTA: What care compels you to say such a thing?

OEDIPUS: I thought I heard you say this: that Laius
was cut down where the three wagon-roads meet.

JOCASTA: So it was announced, nor has it changed at all.

755   OEDIPUS: And where is the place where he suffered this?

JOCASTA: The land is called Phocis, and a split road
leads to it both from Delphi and from Daulia.

OEDIPUS: And how long has passed since these things
happened?

JOCASTA: It was announced in the city just
760   before you took the rule of this land.

OEDIPUS: O Zeus, why have you willed me to do this?

JOCASTA: What is it, Oedipus, that grips your heart?

OEDIPUS: Do not question me further, but tell me:
What did Laius look like, how old was he?

765 JOCASTA: Tall, his hair just sprinkled with white like snow,
    though his figure was not far from yours.

OEDIPUS: Alas, alas! It seems that I have just cast
    myself unknowing under terrible curses!

JOCASTA: Why say that? I tremble to look at you, my lord!

770 OEDIPUS: I am terribly afraid the prophet can see.
    You will prove it, if you tell me one thing further.

JOCASTA: Though I still tremble, I shall speak what you ask me.

OEDIPUS: Did he go with a small escort, or having
    a large bodyguard, as befits a prince?

775 JOCASTA: There were five men in all, among them a herald,
    and a single chariot that carried Laius.

OEDIPUS: Alas! Already matters are clear! Who was it
    who announced these matters to you, my lady?

JOCASTA: A servant, who returned the sole survivor.

780 OEDIPUS: And does he chance to still be at the palace?

JOCASTA: No, indeed. For when he returned from there
    and saw you holding power and Laius lost,
    he grasped my hand and beseeched me to send
    him to the country to tend the flocks, so that
785   he would be far from the sight of this city.
    This I did, for he was worthy, although a slave,
    to take even greater grace than this.

OEDIPUS: How quickly could he return to us here?

790 JOCASTA: He could be here now! But why do you order this?

OEDIPUS: I fear myself, lady, lest I have
    said too much, and so I wish to see him.[77]

[77]i.e., Oedipus now suspects he killed Laius and has called down curses upon himself.

JOCASTA: But he will come! Now, however, I deserve
to learn what holds so badly for you, my lord.

795 OEDIPUS: Nor will you be deprived, when I am gone so far
into expectations. For how could I speak to one
more important than you as I meet such fortune?
My father is Polybus of Corinth,
my mother Merope of the line of Dorus.[78]

800 I was thought the greatest of the citizens there,
before chance befell me, worthy of marvel,
but not worthy, at least, of my energy.
At a banquet a man overwhelmed by drink
called me a fraud in whom I claimed for my father.

805 That day I tried to hold in my anger,
but the next day I went home and asked
my mother and father, and they angrily
treated the insult as the speech of a drunkard.
I rejoiced with them both at this, but still

810 it chafed me always, for the rumor spread far.
Unknown to my mother and father I set out
to Delphi, and Phoebus sent me away
as unworthy of the answers I had sought,
but telling me other terrible, awful things—

815 that I must sleep with my mother, and
that I would bring to light a brood unbearable
for men to see, and that I must be the slayer
of the father who sired me. I heard and fled,
henceforth to share with Corinth only the stars,[79]

820 where I would never see completed
the disgrace of those evil oracles of mine.
In my travels I came to that place
in which you say that your king was lost.
And to you, lady, I shall speak the truth.

825 When traveling near that very triple road,
a herald and a man riding there
in a chariot, like the man you described,
encountered me. Both the one in front
and the old man himself drove me from the road

830 with force. In my anger I struck the driver,[80]

[78]Dorus was one of the oldest forefathers of the Greeks of the Peloponnesus, a peninsula in Southern Greece.

[79]i.e., he will be so far away that Corinth will be connected to him only because it is under the same sky

[80]An important man like Laius would have another slave walking at the head of the team of horses, while Laius stood or sat in the chariot.

turning me off the road, and the old man,
when he saw, watched me as I passed the chariot
and struck me on the head with the two-pronged goad.[81]
But he more than paid for it and soon was struck
835   by the scepter from this very hand,[82] lying
on his back, at once thrown out of the car.
I killed them all. But if that stranger
had some connection with Laius,
who would be more wretched than this man you see?
840   What man would be more hateful to God,
the man whom no man, foreign or citizen,
may receive at home, nor anyone address,
but all must cast from their house? And no other
called down such curses on me than myself!
845   I even stain the dead man's bed with the hands
at which he perished. Am I so evil?
Not entirely unholy? If I must flee,
then in my flight I may neither see my own kin
nor step inside my fatherland, or I must
850   take my mother in marriage and kill my father
Polybus, who raised and sired me. Who would not,
judging these things, say truly in my case
that they come from a cruel divinity?
Never, o holy reverence of the gods,
855   never may I see this day, but I would rather
be blotted out from humanity before
I saw this stain of my doom arrive upon me.

CHORUS: Although these things trouble us, my lord, until
you learn from the one who was present, have hope.

860 OEDIPUS: Indeed, this much of hope is left to me:
only to await that man, the herdsman.

JOCASTA: And what do you want of him, when he appears?

OEDIPUS: I shall tell you; for if he is found saying
the same tale as you, I shall have escaped this woe.

[81] *a stick with two sharp points at one end used to spur the horses.*

[82] *Oedipus would here lift his hand up to show, "this very hand."*

865 JOCASTA: What special tale did you hear from me?

OEDIPUS: You said he reported that brigands
    killed Laius. If, then, he still says the same
    number, I did not kill him, for surely one man
    could not be equal to many.[83] But if he
870   clearly names a single man, a lone traveler,
    then already this deed comes down upon me.

JOCASTA: Yet, know that his account stood thus, and he cannot
    take it back now, for the city heard these things,
    not I alone. But even if he does alter
875   something from his previous story,
    not even thus, my lord, will he bring to
    light Laius' killer truly accomplished,[84]
    who, indeed, Loxias said must die at the hands
    of my child. Yet my poor boy never slew
880   him, but rather perished himself long before.
    And so I would not look to prophecies,
    not here or anywhere else.

OEDIPUS: You reason well, but, nevertheless, send someone
    to fetch the servant, and don't neglect it.

885 JOCASTA: And soon I shall, but let us go inside the house,
    for I would do nothing but that it is your wish.

[Exeunt omnes.]

CHORUS:[85]   Str. 1
    If only fate may find me still acting
    with reverent holiness in words
    and all my deeds, for which lofty laws
890   are ordained, born
    in heaven above, their only
    father Olympus,
    no mortal form of men
    bore them, nor does
895   forgetfulness ever lull them to sleep.
    In them is a great god, who does not grow old.

[83] *ironic, as the play questions just this assumption.*

[84] *i.e., in accordance with the oracle*

[85] *This ode, the play's second stasimon, is notoriously difficult to interpret.*

Ant. 1

Audacity[86] sires the tyrant—audacity, if
filled up rashly with all excess,
neither timely nor useful,

900   scaling the highest eaves
rushes into precipitous necessity
where it suffers from its ill-placed foot.
I pray that God
will never end the struggle

905   that is good for the city.[87]
I will never cease clinging to God as my protector.

Str. 2

But if someone goes
disdainful in hands or speech,
nor fearing Justice,

910   nor revering the seats of the holy gods,
let a bad fate take him,
the wages of unlucky insolence,
unless he reaps his profit justly
and retreats from impious acts,

915   or if he touches untouchable things in his folly.
What man can protect himself, warding
away the shafts of anger when such things happen?
For if deeds like this are honored,
why must I dance?[88]

Ant. 2

920   No longer will I worship
at the inviolate navel of the world,[89]
nor at Abae,[90]
nor ever in the Olympian shrine,[91]
unless these events are made

925   manifestly clear to all mortals.
But, o powerful one, if you are correctly called that,
Zeus, who rule all things, may they not elude
you and your eternal, deathless empire!
For already the old prophecies of Laius

930   are waning and being set aside.
Apollo does not seem to be honored;
faith wanders, lost.

[Handwritten margin note: world is ruled by destiny, denounce prideful men who defy the gods.]

[Handwritten margin note: If Prophecies are wrong, the gods are useless.]

[86]*The Greek word is* hybris; *see glossary for this term*

[87]*This controversial line could refer to the search for the murderers or the struggle between wealthy Greeks to finance public events.*

[88]*Here, the Chorus may break the dramatic illusion by mentioning their own dance, or they may be using "dance" metaphorically to mean "do religious rites."*

[89]*Delphi is called "inviolate" because Apollo defended it from harm, most famously in the Persian attack on the temple in 480 BCE.*

[90]*a major shrine to Apollo*

[91]*a major shrine to Zeus*

[Enter Jocasta from the palace.]

JOCASTA: Lords of this land, the thought came to me
    to supplicate the shrines of the gods, taking
935   in my hands these wreaths and offerings of incense.
    For Oedipus unduly twists his spirit
    with every sort of grief, not like a man
    of reason, judging new matters by the old,
    but whoever talks has him, if he speaks his fears.
940   And so, since my assurances achieve nothing,
    I have come as a suppliant with these tokens,[92]
    to you, Lycean Apollo, for you are nearest,[93]
    so that you will render us unpolluted,
    since now we are all afraid, seeing him
945   so shaken, who is pilot of our ship.[94]

[Enter Messenger from offstage.]

MESSENGER: Could I learn from you, strangers, where lies
    the house of King Oedipus? Or, indeed,
    tell me where he himself is, if you know.

CHORUS: This is his roof; he himself is within, stranger.[95]
950   Here is his wife and mother of his children.

MESSENGER: Then may there be happiness to you, now
    and always, since you are his wedded wife.

JOCASTA: And likewise to you also, stranger, which you earn
    through your welcome words; but explain what
955   you have come needing and what you wish to tell him.

MESSENGER: Good tidings for your house and your lord,
    my lady.

JOCASTA: What tidings are these, and whence have you
    come?

[92]*the flowers and incense, a very suitable offering when blood sacrifice is inappropriate or unavailable*

[93]*She refers to the shrine to Apollo in front of the palace. "Lycean" in Greek brings Apollo to mind as both bringer of light (lyk) and slayer of the wolf (lykos) / protector of the fold.*

[94]*The "ship of state" metaphor is an old one in Greek thought.*

[95]*This is the polite way for Greeks to address one another before names are known; it was considered impolite in heroic culture to ask a name before proper hospitality had been offered.*

MESSENGER: From Corinth. The word I shall speak—at
    first you might
    rejoice; how could you not? But you may also mourn.

960 JOCASTA: What's this? What twofold power do you hold?

MESSENGER: The people of the land of the Isthmus[96]
    make him their king, as it is announced there.

JOCASTA: But why? Does old Polybus no longer rule there?

MESSENGER: No, indeed, for death holds him in the tomb.

965 JOCASTA: What did you say? Polybus is dead, old man?

MESSENGER: If I do not speak the truth, I should die here.

JOCASTA: Maid,[97] won't you go inside as quick as you can,
    and tell the master of these things? O prophecies
    of the gods, where are you? This man Oedipus
970   has long feared and fled lest he kill him, and now
    this very man has died by chance and not by him.

[Enter Oedipus from the palace.]

OEDIPUS: My dearest Jocasta, my wife, why did you
    send for me to come here from the house?

JOCASTA: Listen to this man, and discover in his words
975   where the august prophecies of God have come.

OEDIPUS: But who is he, and why would he speak to me?

JOCASTA: He is from Corinth, announcing that your father
    Polybus is no more, but has perished.

OEDIPUS: What's this, stranger? You yourself tell me.

[96]*the thin bridge of land connecting the mainland, on which Thebes and Delphi were located, to the Peloponnesus, where Corinth was*

[97]*She addresses one of her attendants, who would be on stage as mute characters.*

980 MESSENGER: If I must state this exactly to you first,
　　　　know well that the man is gone, deceased.

OEDIPUS: By treachery, or meeting some disease?

MESSENGER: A small turn of the scale lays old bodies to rest.

OEDIPUS: Destroyed by disease, it seems, the poor man.

985 MESSENGER: Yes, and by the long measuring of his years.

OEDIPUS: Well, well! Why, my wife, would anyone look
　　　　to the prophesying hearth of Pytho or to
　　　　the shrieking birds above, under whose guidance
　　　　I was to kill my own father? But, he died
990　　and sleeps below the earth; and I am here,
　　　　without touching a spear—unless somehow he
　　　　perished from longing for me, and thus died by me.
　　　　But still, Polybus has taken those prophecies
　　　　as they are—worthless—with him and lies in Hades.

995 JOCASTA: Did I not predict it thus earlier?

OEDIPUS: You did, but I was led by my fear.

JOCASTA: Now, then, toss none of these matters in your heart.

OEDIPUS: And how can I not dread my mother's bed?

JOCASTA: Why should a person fear when the ways of fortune
1000　　are supreme, when there is no clear foresight?
　　　　It's best to live at random, however one can.
　　　　Do not worry you will wed your mother,
　　　　for many mortals already have lain with
　　　　their mothers in dreams. Rather, the one for whom
1005　　these things are nothing bears life easiest.

OEDIPUS: All these matters you would explain well,
　　　　if my mother were dead; but since she lives,
　　　　I must fear, however prettily you speak.

JOCASTA: Surely your father's tomb is also a bright sign?[98]

1010 OEDIPUS: Bright, I agree, but my fear is of her who lives.

MESSENGER: And who is this woman who so frightens you?

OEDIPUS: Merope, old man, with whom Polybus lived.

MESSENGER: But what in her moves you to such fear?

OEDIPUS: A terrible prophecy sent by God, stranger.

1015 MESSENGER: Tell me—or is it lawful that another know?

OEDIPUS: Certainly: Loxias once told me
        that I must sleep with my own mother and
        shed paternal blood with my own hands.
        Thus for a long time I have kept Corinth
1020   far from me—and prosperously, but still
        your parents' eyes are the sweetest thing to see.

MESSENGER: Dreading those things, then, you are exiled
           from that place?

OEDIPUS: And wishing not to murder my father, old man!

MESSENGER: Why, then, have I not freed you from this fear,
1025   my lord, since indeed I come in good will?

OEDIPUS: Indeed, you would take deserved grace from me.

MESSENGER: I came for this very purpose, so that when you
           returned home I would have done well by you!

OEDIPUS: But I will never go where my parents are!

1030 MESSENGER: O child, you clearly do not know what you do.

OEDIPUS: How's that, old man? By the gods, teach me!

[98]*Literally, " a big eye," the eye being conceived as something bright and comforting. It is also a metaphor rich with irony for this play.*

MESSENGER: If it is because of this you flee your home…

OEDIPUS: I dread that Phoebus accomplish these things for me.

MESSENGER: Or that you might take pollution from your parents?

1035 OEDIPUS: This very thing, old sir, has ever been my fear.

MESSENGER: Don't you know you may justly fear nothing?

OEDIPUS: How so, if I am the child of those parents?

MESSENGER: Because Polybus is nothing to you by birth!

OEDIPUS: How can you say this? Did Polybus not sire me?

1040 MESSENGER: You have nothing from him, no more than from me.

OEDIPUS: How can my father be equal to nothing?

MESSENGER: That man did not beget you, no more than I!

OEDIPUS: But then…why did he call me his child?

MESSENGER: Know that he took you as a gift from my own arms.

1045 OEDIPUS: And still he loved me greatly, though not his own?

MESSENGER: His former childlessness persuaded him.

OEDIPUS: But you—had you purchased me or found me by chance?

MESSENGER: I found you in the woody glens of Cithaeron.

OEDIPUS: Why were you traveling in that place?

1050 MESSENGER: At that time I had the care of mountain flocks.

OEDIPUS: Why, you were a shepherd, a nomad for hire?

MESSENGER: And also at that time, my child, your savior.

OEDIPUS: What misfortune was mine when you found me?

MESSENGER: Your ankles should testify to that.

1055 OEDIPUS: Oh, why must you mention that old affliction?

MESSENGER: I freed you when your feet were pierced at
        the ankles.

OEDIPUS: Such terrible disgrace I took from my cradle.

MESSENGER: Such that you were named from this misfortune.[99]

OEDIPUS: Tell me, by god, from my mother or father?

1060 MESSENGER: I don't know; he who gave you to me would
        know this.

OEDIPUS: You took me from someone, didn't find me yourself?

MESSENGER: No, another shepherd gave you to me.

OEDIPUS: Who was he? Could you describe him clearly?

MESSENGER: I believe he was called one of Laius' people.

1065 OEDIPUS: The former king of this very land?

MESSENGER: Exactly—he was a herdsman of that man.

OEDIPUS: And is this man still alive, so I could see him?

[99]*"Oedipus" means "swollen feet."*

MESSENGER: You who live here would know that better
  than I.

OEDIPUS: Does anyone standing here now know
1070   the herdsman of whom he speaks? You might
    have seen him in the fields or even here! Tell me,
    for now it is time for this to be learned at last![100]

CHORUS: I know of none other than the one from the fields
    whom you wanted to see earlier, but
1075   Jocasta here could say these things best of all.

OEDIPUS: Lady, do you know that man, whom just now
  we summoned? Is he the one this man speaks of?

JOCASTA: What does it matter whom he means? Ignore it.[101]
  Don't think about it—it will all end in vain.

1080 OEDIPUS: It is impossible that when I have found
    such signs, I will not discover my birth.

JOCASTA: No, by the gods! If indeed you care for your
  own life, do not go after this! I grieve enough.

OEDIPUS: Cheer up, for even if I am revealed a slave
1085   three generations back, you will not be proved base.[102]

JOCASTA: All the same, obey me, I pray. Do not do this.

OEDIPUS: I cannot be persuaded not to learn this clearly.

JOCASTA: Yet I understand it well—what I say is best.

OEDIPUS: What you say is best has long annoyed me.

1090 JOCASTA: Unlucky man, may you never know who you are!

OEDIPUS: Will someone go and bring the shepherd to me?
  Let this one rejoice in her own rich birth.

[100]Note Oedipus'
great excitement
to finally end the
mystery surround-
ing his birth.

[101]Jocasta, of
course, has real-
ized the truth.

[102]Oedipus misun-
derstands Jocasta's
concerns. He
thinks she is wor-
ried because if he
is found to be of
servile birth, then
she, a princess,
will have married
a slave. He has
no idea she is his
mother.

JOCASTA: Alas, alas—unhappy man! This alone can
   I say to you, and nothing else ever after.

   [Exit Jocasta into the palace.]

1095 CHORUS: Why ever did your wife go away,
   Oedipus, stirred by wild grief? I fear that
   something evil will burst out from that silence.

   OEDIPUS: Let it all burst out, if it must! As for me,
   though it be small, I wish to know my stock.
1100 But she, since a woman is proud of such things,
   she is troubled by this low birth of mine.
   But I deem myself the child of Chance,
   who gives good things, and I will not be dishonored.
   She is my mother, and my brothers,
1105 the Months, have seen me both small and great.[103]
   Being born what I am, I could never be
   another, so I should seek out my descent.

   CHORUS:[104]   *Str.*
   If I am a prophet
   and wise with intelligence,
1110 by heaven, o Cithaeron, you will surely know
   at tomorrow's full moon
   that you are the fellow countryman of Oedipus
   and, as nurse and mother, made him grow.
   We will sing and dance for you,
1115 for you have served our kings!
   Hail, Phoebus, to you also
   may these things be pleasing.

                                                 Ant.
   Who bore you, child,
   which of the long-lived maids[105]
1120 was the mountain-ranging bride of Pan?[106]
   for to him all the beast-pasturing highlands are dear.
   Perhaps the lord of Cyllene[107]
   or the Bacchic god[108]
   who dwells on mountain tops,
1125 will accept you, foundling,

[103]Oedipus declares himself the child of Tyche (Chance); the children of Tyche are the Months, which symbolize changes throughout the year. Hence, they have noted the change in Oedipus' personal fortunes; see Tyche.

[104]This ode, the third stasimon, is very short; the Chorus are ecstatically carried away by Oedipus' declaration. In return, they declare him of divine origin. The consequent raising of their hopes contributes to the complete ruin into which everyone will crash in the next episode.

[105]the Nymphs, who were often thought of not as immortal goddesses, but merely as living long beyond the span of mortal men.

[106]the goat-legged god of wild things and places; hence his favorite places are the pastures of 'beasts' and not sheep, cattle, or other domestic animals.

[107]Hermes

[108]Dionysus

from one of the glancing-eyed nymphs,
with whom he plays most of all.

OEDIPUS:[109] If I must surmise the identity of one
I've never met, aged sirs, I think I see
1130   the shepherd we have long been seeking. For measured
by his great old age he could be this man,
and moreover those leading him I know as
my own servants; but you should have surer
knowledge than I, as you've seen the man before.

[Enter Shepherd.]

1135   CHORUS: Yes, I recognize him. Know it clearly, for if
any man were Laius' trusted shepherd, it's him.

OEDIPUS: First I will ask you, the Corinthian stranger,
is this the man you meant?

MESSENGER: That very man you see.

1140   OEDIPUS: You there, old man, look at me and say
whatever I ask you: Were you once Laius' man?

SHEPHERD: Yes, his slave, not purchased, but born to his
house.

OEDIPUS: What work and what livelihood was your care?

SHEPHERD: For most of my life I have followed flocks.

1145   OEDIPUS: In what regions did you live most of the time?

SHEPHERD: Sometimes Cithaeron, sometimes places near it.

OEDIPUS: Did you see this man at some point and know him?

SHEPHERD: See him doing what? Who are you talking about?

OEDIPUS: This one who's here! Have you ever met him?

1150 SHEPHERD: Not such that my memory quickly answers yes.

MESSENGER: This, at least, is nothing strange, master, but I
 clearly remember him; and I know well that
 he remembers when that same spot on Cithaeron
 he grazed with two flocks and I with one.
1155 I was his neighbor there three whole times,
 six months apiece, from spring to autumn.
 Then in winter I drove my flocks to the
 fold and he to the stables of Laius.
 Didn't it happen just like I said?

1160 SHEPHERD: You speak the truth, although a long time has passed.

MESSENGER: Then say now, do you remember giving me then
 a child to raise for myself as my foster-son?

SHEPHERD: What does it matter? Why do you ask this question?

MESSENGER: Here is that man, my friend, who was so little
 then![110]

[110]*He indicates Oedipus.*

1165 SHEPHERD: Go to hell! Will you not be silent?

OEDIPUS: Ah! Do not reproach him, old man, when
 your words deserve more reproach than him.

SHEPHERD: But what, o best of masters, have I done wrong?

OEDIPUS: You do not discuss the child whom he researches.

1170 SHEPHERD: Because he speaks without knowing, but acts in vain.

OEDIPUS: If you'll not speak for my favor, you'll speak in pain!

SHEPHERD: By the gods, surely you will not hurt an old man!

OEDIPUS: Quickly—someone twist back this man's arms![111]

SHEPHERD: Unhappy me! Why? What do you desire to learn?

1175 OEDIPUS: Did you give him the child he mentioned?

SHEPHERD: I did, but I should have died that day!

OEDIPUS: If you don't talk, you'll come to that today!

SHEPHERD: I will be destroyed even more if I do talk.

OEDIPUS: This man, it seems, is trying to stall.

1180 SHEPHERD: No, no! I said long ago that I did give it.

OEDIPUS: Where did you get it? From your house or
            another's?

SHEPHERD: It was not mine, but I took it from another.

OEDIPUS: From one of the citizens here, and from what
            house?

SHEPHERD: By the gods, master, do not inquire further!

1185 OEDIPUS: You are dead if I have to ask it again!

SHEPHERD: Then...he was from the house of Laius.

OEDIPUS: A slave, or one born to his family?

SHEPHERD: Oh, I am about to say something terrible.

OEDIPUS: And I to hear it, but still it must be heard!

1190 SHEPHERD: He was said to be the child of that man himself,
            but your wife could explain the situation best.

[111] to prepare him for a flogging

OEDIPUS: Because she gave it to you?

SHEPHERD: Yes, my lord.

OEDIPUS: To what end?

1195 SHEPHERD: So that I would kill it.

OEDIPUS: Its mother dared this?

SHEPHERD: Fearing evil prophecies.

OEDIPUS: What were they?

SHEPHERD: That he would kill his parents.

1200 OEDIPUS: Why, then, did you entrust him to this old man?

SHEPHERD: Out of pity, master. It seemed he would bear him
     away to another land, his home. But he
     rescued him into the greatest evils. For if
     you are who he says, know that you were born cursed.

1205 OEDIPUS: Alas, alas. It's all come out so clearly.
     Light, let me see the last of you now,
     surrounded by those I ought to avoid—
     born from them, living with them, killing them.
                              [*Exit Oedipus into the palace.*[112]]

CHORUS:[113]   *Str. 1*
     Oh, the generations of man—
1210   while you live, I count you
     as worthless, equal to nothing.
     For who, what man
     wins more happiness than
     just its shape
1215   and the ruin when that shape collapses?
     With your example, your fate, your self,
     suffering Oedipus,
     I call nothing of mortals blessed.

[112]*The Messenger and the Shepherd might go offstage at any point after this; without stage directions, however, we cannot be sure when.*

[113]*The fourth stasimon places Oedipus' downfall in the context of all human existence. The theme is one common in 5th century BCE Greek thought, a traditional moral that became almost an obsession in authors like Sophocles and Herodotus: call no man happy until he is dead.*

Ant. 1

He shot with unsurpassed aim

1220　and gained every kind of

happiness, o Zeus; destroying

the riddle-singer,

the maiden with twisted talons,

like a tower

1225　he stood and defended my land from death.

Since that time he has been called my king

and beyond all men

was honored, ruling in glorious Thebes.

Str. 2

But now, who could be called

1230　more wretched, more bound to toil and wild madness,

more the paradigm of life's reversals?

Oh, famous Oedipus,

you alone sufficed to lie

as son, father, and bridegroom;

1235　how was it, how, poor man,

could your paternal furrows[114]

bear you in such long silence?

Ant. 2

All-seeing time discovered you unwilling,

it judged long ago your marriage that is no marriage,

1240　you, both the siring and sired.

Alas, o child of Laius,

if only, if only we had never

set eyes on you!

My grief is like a libation[115] poured from my mouth.

1245　But to speak the truth, because of you I could breathe
　　　　again

and because of you I sink my eyes into sleep.[116]

[Enter Servant from the palace.]

SERVANT:[117] Gentlemen, of this land always the most honored,

what deeds you shall hear, what deeds you shall see,
　　　　and what

grief you will take upon yourselves, if you still care

[114]*sexual*

[115]*a liquid sacri-
fice, most often
of wine, perfume,
milk, honey,
or a combina-
tion. These were
given in many
circumstances, but
especially were
poured at tombs to
the shades of the
dead.*

[116]*a reference to
Oedipus' saving
of the city and his
destruction*

[117]*the "Second
Messenger" of
the play, who
rushes out of the
palace to narrate
the events within.
The language is
starkly vivid; no
emotional power
is lost by the
audience's not
seeing the events
narrated.*

1250   as kin for the house of the Labdacids.
        For I think that neither the Danube nor Volga
        could wash through this house to purify all
        it conceals, but soon will come into the light
        evils both willing and unwilling, but even
1255   the self-chosen of these pains will grieve you greatly.

CHORUS: What we knew before did not fail to be
        grievous, but what will you say in addition?

SERVANT: It is the fastest of words both to say and
        to learn: Our divine queen, Jocasta, is dead.

1260 CHORUS: O poor woman! By whatever cause?

SERVANT: By herself! But, of what has been done the worst pain
        you will avoid, for you cannot see it.
        Still, as much as I can remember
        of that poor woman's woes you shall learn.
1265   After she had gone into her chamber, frenzied,
        she threw herself onto her bridal couch,
        snatching at her hair with both hands.[118] Bolting the doors
        from the inside, she called on Laius, so long
        a corpse, remembering that ancient creation,
1270   by which he himself died and left her, as mother,
        to his offspring for their own evil brood.
        She groaned over her bed, where twice doomed she had
        born husband from husband, children from her child.
        When she died, I do not know; for Oedipus
1275   burst in shouting, and so we did not note her doom,
        but were looking at him, ranging about.
        He paced back and forth, asking us to bring a sword,
        asking where she had gone, his wife who was no wife,
        but a doubly-ploughed field, mother of him
1280   and his children. Some god led him on,
        for it was none of us men who were nearby;
        shouting terribly, as if led there by some guide,
        he was driven to the doors, and from their sockets
        he forced the groaning bolts and fell into the room.

[118]*Tearing one's hair was a traditional sign of mourning for Greek women.*

1285   Then inside we saw the woman hanging,
        all twisted up in a twisted noose.
        When he saw her, the wretch shouted awfully
        and cut her down from the noose. When she lay
        on the ground, poor thing, it was terrible to see.
1290   For he removed from her garment the golden
        brooches which she was wearing; he lifted them
        and struck the sockets of his own eyes,
        shouting that they would not see either the evils
        he had suffered or the evils he had done,
1295   now only in darkness could they see those whom
        they must not see, in darkness could they mistake
        those whom they wanted to recognize.
        Repeating these things, many times and not once
        only he raised his hands and struck his eyes. At once
1300   his bloody eyeballs moistened his cheeks.
        In torrent together flowed the drops of blood;
        all at once a dark storm of blood like hail rained down.
        From two, not one alone, these evils burst forth,
        evils wedded together for husband and wife.
1305   Their old happiness that was before was justly
        called happiness, but now on this one day
        mourning, madness, death, disgrace, every way
        to name all evils—none have been absent.

CHORUS: Does the poor wretch now have some rest from evil?

1310 SERVANT: He shouts at us to open the doors and reveal
        to all the people of Cadmus the parricide,
        and his mother's...what he said I will not repeat.
        He wants to cast himself from the land and not
        stay at home accursed with his own curses.
1315   He lacks, however, strength and a guide,
        for the pain is greater than he can bear.
        But he will show you also, for the doors
        are opening. Soon you will see a sight
        that even his enemy would pity.

[119]*unusual for a Greek tragedy; the actor playing Oedipus will have changed masks—the new mask would have shown Oedipus' blindness in a gory way.*

[Enter Oedipus from the palace with attendants.[119]]

1320 CHORUS:[120] O suffering terrible for men to see,
    o most terrible of all I have
    encountered! What mania, poor wretch,
    stood by you? What spirit
    leapt from beyond the highest places
1325   onto your unhappy fate?[121]
    Alas, alas, unfortunate man,
    I cannot look at you,
    though I wish to ask many things, ·
    to learn and ponder them;
1330   how you make me shudder and fear!

OEDIPUS: Ah! Ah! How miserable is my life!
    Where does my pain take me?
    How does my voice rush about me?
    O doom, how you've pounced!

1335 CHORUS: Onto horror that can neither be heard nor viewed.
                              Str. 1

OEDIPUS: Oh, darkness!
    This cloud of mine, abominable, approaching ineffable,
    unconquered, driven on by a fatally favorable wind.
    Sorrow!
1340   And still more sorrow—Upon me fall together
    so many stinging goads and the memory of evils.

CHORUS: And it is no wonder that in such woes
    you suffer doubly and doubly cry aloud.
                              Ant. 1

OEDIPUS: Oh, my friend!
1345   You are still my only companion, for
    still you remain by me, tending the blind man.
    Sorrow!
    For I have not missed your presence, but, although
    in darkness, I recognize your voice clearly.

1350 CHORUS: O agent of terrors, how could you dare to
    put out[122] your eyes like that? What god set you to it?

[120]*Here begins the kommos between the Chorus and Oedipus. While Oedipus speaks in lyric meters, the Chorus speak only in iambic lines, the normal meter of dialogue. This contrasts Oedipus' heightened emotional state with the Chorus' more deliberate response.*

[121]*Greek poetry often portrays evil spirits in high places (dancing on the rooftops, for instance), preparing to pounce upon their victims.*

[122]*Sophocles uses a word for extinguishing a fire; sight and eyes, in Greek, are often described as lights, and Oedipus has snuffed his out.*

Str. 2

OEDIPUS: Apollo, my friends—these things are Apollo,
who brought to pass these evil, evil sufferings of mine.
But no man struck me with his hand,
1355   but I myself dared it.
For why must I see,
I for whom no sight is sweet?

CHORUS: Indeed, it is as you say.

OEDIPUS: What, then, could be worth seeing to me,
1360   or lovable, what word addressed to me
could I hear gladly, friends?
Lead me into exile quickly,
lead me away, friends, completely destroyed,
the most accursed, and to the gods
1365   the most hated of men!

CHORUS: Equally wretched in your mind and your
misfortune, how I wish I had never known you.

Ant. 2

OEDIPUS: Let him die who took off the fierce fetters,
feeding off my feet, and rescued and saved
1370   me from my death, no good deed for me!
For if I had died then,
I would not have brought
so much pain to my friends or me!

CHORUS: It is my wish, too, that it have been thus.

1375 OEDIPUS: I'd not then be my father's slayer,
nor called the groom of her whence I was born.
Abandoned by the gods, child of sacrilege,
sharing the source of those I myself sired.
Were some evil greater still than evil,
1380   this, too, would be Oedipus' lot.[123]

CHORUS: I do not know how to agree with your judgment,
for you are better not living than living blind.

[123]*This is the last line of the kommos.*

OEDIPUS: Do not tell me that these things were not
    done well, nor offer me further counsel.
1385   For I don't know with what eyes I could look
    and see my father when I go down to Hell,[124]
    nor again my poor mother; to those two
    my deeds are beyond what hanging could punish.
    Or is the sight of my children desirable
1390   for me to see, sprouting as they sprouted?
    Surely never to those eyes of mine!
    Nor the city nor citadel, nor the holy
    shrines of the gods, from which I, the worst of men,
    removed myself, myself decreeing
1395   that all expel the impious one, revealed
    unholy by the gods and, now, of Laius' race.
    Exposing such defilement as this,
    did I intend to see them with my own eyes?
    Not at all. Rather if I could somehow block
1400   my hearing from the ears, I would not hold back
    from fully shutting off this wretched frame of mine,
    so that I'd be blind and hear nothing, for to live
    outside comprehension of these woes would be sweet.
    Oh, Cithaeron! Why did you accept me? Why did
1405   you not kill me at once, so that I would never
    reveal to men my origins? O Polybus
    and Corinth and my old ancestral home—
    so-called—in what a pretty festering
    of evils you brought me up! For now I
1410   find myself evil and born from evil people.
    O three paths and hidden groves and the
    narrow oak coppice at the triple crossroads,
    which drank my own blood from my father
    from my own hands, do you still remember me?
1415   What deeds I performed in your presence,
    what deeds I was still to do! O marriage, marriage,
    you brought me forth, and afterwards again
    you harvested that same seed and revealed
    father-brothers, children of kin blood,
1420   brides who were wives and mothers, and all else
    counted the most shameful acts by men.

[124]*The Greeks did not distinguish a separate afterlife for the good or bad. All the dead went to the same gloomy fate: not torture, but a bleak, barren eternity with neither light nor sweetness.*

But, since these matters are as foully said as done,
by the gods, quickly hide me from the sight of men
somehow, or kill me or cast me into the sea,
1425   where you will never see me again.
Go, deem it worthy to touch a poor man!
Yield, do not fear; for my evils are
such that no one of men can bear but me.

CHORUS: No, Creon is here, the right one to decide
1430   whether to act or advise on what you ask; since
he alone remains to guard our land in your stead.

[Enter Creon from offstage.]

OEDIPUS: Alas! What can I say to this man?
What real faith can he have in me? For in all
that went before I am found false to him.

1435 CREON: I have not come to mock you, Oedipus,
nor to scold you for some previous wrong.
                  [He addresses the attendants.]
But you, if you feel no shame before the races
of men, then revere at least the nourishing
light of lord Helios,[125] and do not thus
1440   show this blight unconcealed, which neither
earth nor holy rain nor light accept.
Take him into the house as quick as you can,
for it is right for only blood relatives
to see and hear familial evils.

1455 OEDIPUS: By the gods, since you've cheated my
          expectations[126]
and come as the best of men to me, the worst,
grant me this; I ask for you and not for me.

CREON: What is this thing you need so greatly?

OEDIPUS: Cast me immediately from this land,
1450   somewhere I can avoid all mortal speech.

[125]*the Sun*

[126]*i.e., that Creon came to mock or take revenge on Oedipus*

CREON: Know well that I would do this, but first I
must learn from the god what must be done.

OEDIPUS: But his entire prophecy was made clear;
destroy the patricide, the accursed, me!

1455 CREON: It was said thus, but still, where we stand
it is better to learn what must be done.

OEDIPUS: You would ask on behalf of one so wretched?

CREON: Yes, for now even you should bear faith to the god.

OEDIPUS: Then I enjoin you and make this request:
1460   to her...who is inside[127]...bury her as you will,
rightly will you act on behalf of your own—
but as for me, may this, my native city,
suffer me to dwell here while I live,
but let me to dwell in the mountains, with my own
1465   famous Cithaeron, which my mother and
father while they lived appointed as my tomb,
so that I may die as those two wished.
Although this much at least I know: No disease
nor anything else can kill me, for I would not
1470   have been saved from death, but for some dire fate.
This destiny of mine, let it go where it may,
but for my children, Creon—don't worry
over my sons; they are men, so that
they will never lack a livelihood, wherever
1475   they may be. But, for my poor little girls,
they've not so much as eaten a meal
apart from me; but whatever I touched,
those two always had a share in all of it.
Worry over them, and most of all I beg you,
1480   let me touch them with my hands and mourn our woes.
Please, my lord![128]
Please, o truly noble man, could my hands touch them,
I'd think I held them as I did when I could see.

[127]*He cannot bring himself to say her name or her relation to him.*

[128]*Sophocles shows Oedipus' emotion by puncturing the longer, ordinary speech with short lines.*

[129]Oedipus' daugh-
ters, Antigone and
Ismene, played
an important role
in the traditional
stories about
the aftermath of
Oedipus' down-
fall, particu-
larly in Sophocles'
Antigone.

[Servants lead onstage the two girls.[129]]

What's this now?

1485 By the gods, do I somehow hear my two dear girls
crying? Has Creon pitied me and
sent to me the dearest of my offspring?
Is it true?

CREON: You are, for I am the one who prepared these things,
1490   knowing the joy they have long brought you.

OEDIPUS: Then may you be blessed, and for this meeting
may fate guard you better than it did me!
My children, where are you? Come here, come
to these hands of mine that are siblings to yours,
1495   hands that brought to this sad state the once
bright eyes of your begetting father,
who, children, neither seeing nor knowing was
proved your father from the same place he himself
sprang.
And I weep for you, although I cannot see you;
1500   contemplating the bitterness of your lives,
the sort of life men will force you to live.
What sort of company will you keep in town?
What festivals will you attend that will not
send you home in tears, instead of joy?[130]
1505   When you come to the age ripe for marriage,
who will he be who will run the risk, children,
to take for himself the reproaches that will
be banes for my parents and offspring alike?
What evil is absent? Your father
1510   slew his father; he ploughed his mother,
where he himself was sown, and he sired
you in the same fount where he himself was sired.
Such taunts you will hear, and then who will marry you?
There is no one, my children, but surely
1515   you must die untilled and unmarried.
Son of Menoeceus, since you alone are left
as father to them, for we who created them

[130]Because of the
curse now on their
house, the girls
cannot take part
in the religious
festivals that
made up the bulk
of Greek social
life; their presence
would pollute the
festival and avert
the gods' favor.

have both been destroyed, do not allow them,
your kin, to die unwed and beggars,
1520   nor make them party to my evils;
but pity them, seeing how young they are
and bereft of everything, except for you.
Consent, noble one, and touch me with your hand.
Oh, children, if you could understand, I would
1525   give you so much advice; as it is, just pray
with me that you obtain a better life
than did the father who sired you.

CREON: You have gone far enough in weeping; go inside.

OEDIPUS: I will, though sadly.

1530 CREON: All things are fair in time.

OEDIPUS: Do you know my conditions?

CREON: Speak; I shall learn them.

OEDIPUS: Send me from this land.

CREON: You ask me what is God's to give.

1535 OEDIPUS: The gods hate me.

CREON: Then they will grant your wish.

OEDIPUS: Then you will do it?

CREON: I'll say only what I think.

OEDIPUS: Then lead me away.

1540 CREON: Come, let go of the children.

OEDIPUS: Do not take them from me!

CREON: It is not your place to decide;
the power you had has not remained with you.

[*Exeunt Creon and Oedipus with the attendants and children into the palace.*]

CHORUS: People of our country Thebes, behold this
                Oedipus,
1545   who knew the famous riddle and was a most powerful
        man,
        whose fortunes all the citizens watched with emulation,
        how deep the sea of dire misfortune that has taken him!
        Therefore, it is necessary to call no man blessed
1550   as we await the final day, until he has reached
        the limit of life and suffered nothing grievous.

Mythological Background

Greek tragedies were based on widely-known myths or famous historical events, so the audience would know the characters and outline of the story they were about to see. Seeing a play about Oedipus, for instance, Sophocles' Athenian audience would already know that this story came from the cycle of myths about the city of Thebes, one of Athens' rivals in the 5th century. Most surprises did not come from the plot, but from the new way the playwright used familiar material.

The Oedipus story is set a few generations before the Trojan War, which the ancient Greeks placed in 1184 BCE. King Laius of Thebes received a prophecy that his son would kill him. To avoid the outcome of the prophecy, Laius had his baby *exposed* (abandoned without protection from the elements—a common way to get rid of unwanted infants) on Mount Cithaeron, one of the most remote points of his kingdom. As an extra precaution, he nailed the child's feet together. Unfortunately for Laius, the baby survived and was raised as a prince of the city of Corinth. He was named Oedipus, which means "swollen feet" in Greek.

Many years later, Oedipus, not knowing his true birth, met Laius on the road and killed him. At the time, Thebes was being terrorized by a monster with the head of a woman, body of a lion, and wings of an eagle called the Sphinx. She was particularly famous for telling everyone she encountered a riddle: "What walks on four legs in the morning, two legs in the afternoon, and three legs in the evening?" Men who answered incorrectly were devoured.

Oedipus answered the challenge by guessing "man" (who crawls as a baby, walks on two legs as an adult, and leans on a cane in his old age). Her riddle solved, the Sphinx threw herself from a cliff, and Oedipus was crowned king of Thebes. Oedipus married the recently widowed queen, Jocasta. He did not know his real relationship to the man he killed and the woman he married.

Because Sophocles' audience was already familiar with this information, he does not need to explain it in the drama; he can simply allude to it.

The Origins of Greek Drama

We do not know much about the origin of Greek theater. The plays that survive all date from the 5th century BCE, but tragedy had been performed in Athens for at least decades before the earliest play, and the actual roots of drama reach even farther back. The word *drama* itself comes from a verb meaning "to do" or "to act." Thus, a *drama* is simply something acted. The two most important influences on Athenian drama were the epics of Homer and the tradition of narrative lyric poetry performed by large Choruses.

Homer and Epic Poems

The ancient Greeks traced all their literary traditions back to the author of two epic poems, the *Iliad* and the *Odyssey*. Although we now know that these were the products of an oral tradition, the Greeks believed that the blind poet Homer had written both works. The *Iliad*, which narrates just a little of the Trojan War, was considered by the philosopher Aristotle to be the parent of tragedy, and very many Greek tragedies took their subject matter from the heroes portrayed in the *Iliad*. Although they do not survive, other epic poems told the myths of the city of Thebes and the fall of its ruling house—the subject matter of the *Oedipus Rex*.

Lyric Poetry

While tragedy takes much of its subject matter from epic, its closest relatives in form were the long lyric poems sung by large Choruses. In fact, some scholars have speculated that the Chorus leader of the lyric poems evolved into a main character, then was replaced by a new Chorus leader; the final result could have been a form with a Chorus, Chorus leader, and main character. Dialogue arising between these three speakers may have grown into the dramatic action of the first Greek plays.

It is interesting to note that the lyric poems continued to be an important form in their own right even as drama became popular. At the Great Dionysia, one of the major festivals of Athens, performance of the dithyramb (a special kind of lyric poem dedicated to the god Dionysus) was as important as the performance of plays. Each of the ten tribes of Athens submitted an entry in the contest and was represented by a Chorus of up to fifty men.

Tragedy and the City

Fifth century Athens saw advances in philosophy, rhetoric, literature, science, architecture, and the visual arts; it was a time of almost unparalleled cultural achievement. Tragedy was the premiere literary genre of this period, and it is fitting that the high point of the democracy should be symbolized by a genre of poetry that involves the entire body of citizens. Performed at one of the major festivals of the city, the Great Dionysia, each tragedy was part of a contest. Three playwrights would be chosen by a city official, and each playwright would produce three tragedies and a satyr-play (a kind of farce intended to lighten the mood after three tragedies); all four plays were performed in a single day. The audience consisted of about 15,000 citizens, and the festival itself became a pageant of Athenian power and glory.

We know of many playwrights from this century, but only the works of three men have survived. Fortunately, the three poets we have were universally considered to be the best: Aeschylus, Sophocles, and Euripides. From Sophocles, who won twenty victories (compared to Aeschylus' thirteen and Euripides' four) we have the seven plays chosen by ancient critics as his finest: *Ajax, The Women of Trachis, Electra, Philoctetes,* and the so-called "Theban plays," *Oedipus Tyrannus, Oedipus at Colonus,* and *Antigone*. These three plays are not a trilogy; they were not written in order or performed together at one festival. In fact, about forty years separates the first play written, *Antigone*, from the last, *Oedipus at Colonus*! Each play, therefore, should be considered a separate work, and while Sophocles alludes to his earlier work, he pursued different goals and used different methods for each one.

Conventions of Greek Drama

The most important convention of the Greek stage was the wearing of masks with attached wigs by all performers. The elaborate costumes worn by the actors and Chorus members were often the most striking visual element. Staging was usually limited to the painted background behind the stage. Greek tragedies are all set outside, so this background usually depicted the exterior of the main characters' residence—in the case of the *Oedipus Rex*, the palace of Oedipus and the shrine to Apollo in front of it. The action of a Greek tragedy takes place in a single day, so changes of scene are rare, and props are kept to a minimum. In addition to the Chorus and the three actors, mute characters could also appear on stage as needed. In front of the stage, which was not raised from the ground as in modern theaters, was a circular area called the *orchestra*, in which the Chorus performed its dances. These would be accompanied by the music of an *aulos,* a double pipe similar to a modern oboe.

The plays followed a fairly strict structure, with a prologue, the entrance of the Chorus, and then several episodes separated by choral odes. The dialogue of the plays is written in meter, but was spoken, like the plays of Shakespeare, whereas the choral odes were written in a more complicated meter for the Chorus to sing and dance. The plays also include a *kommos*, in which the main character(s) lament in song with the Chorus. All in all, the form of Greek tragedy somewhat resembles a cross between Shakespeare and opera. It is important for modern readers to remember that, without the benefit of any music or the elaborate costumes and scenery, we are getting a small portion of what the original audience received.

Aristotle's Influence on Our Understanding of Tragedy

Aristotle was a great 4th century BCE philosopher who spent much of his life in Athens. He wrote one of the earliest and most important pieces of literary criticism, the *Poetics*. It is important to note, however, that the ideas about tragedy expressed in the *Poetics* were not necessarily held by the playwrights themselves, and most tragedies do not fit the strict guidelines established by Aristotle. The *Poetics* is the origin of the "tragic hero" concept, but in many tragedies, it is hard to figure out exactly who this tragic hero is. We should not hold a play to a philosopher's standard, and just because Aristotle says something about tragedy or a specific play does not make it true. In general, the influence of the *Poetics* on future scholars has been somewhat excessive.

Aristotle can, nevertheless, help us understand how these plays were read and received about by the ancient Greeks themselves. *Oedipus Rex* was the tragedy that most closely fit his guidelines. Oedipus is the model of the "tragic hero," because the concept is based on him. Because of his *hamartia* (mistake), he suffers a *peripeteia* (reversal), which, for Aristotle, is the heart of tragedy. Although *hamartia* is often translated as "tragic flaw," there is debate among scholars as to the nature and scale of the error that causes a tragic hero's downfall. Some interpret the term to mean a mere accident or mistake of perception that may or may not be related to a moral weakness in the hero's character. The *peripeteia* we might call a "reversal of fortune," and in most tragedies, we do see the protagonists change from better to worse circumstances.

For Aristotle, this reversal was the key towards rousing fear and pity in the audience, which led to *catharsis,* another term that has become widely used in the study of literature. A word from Greek religion, *catharsis* indicates ritual purification from pollution, an important concept for Greek life. This pollution, or *miasma*, came about as the result of crime, especially murder. Just as the physical blood spilled had to be cleaned up, so the more abstract *miasma* needed to be purified through the proper rituals. This applied to the space where the crime occurred and to the person who committed it; if a murderer went somewhere without being purified, he would bring pollution onto this new place. This is precisely the situation at the beginning of *Oedipus Rex,* in which the gods have sent a plague against Thebes because of the presence of Laius' murderer in the city and because of the incest of Oedipus and Jocasta.

Aristotle uses the term *catharsis* to refer to the purging of excessive emotions from a person. By watching the tragedy and feeling the strong emotions of fear and pity on behalf of the characters on stage, the spectator experiences a kind of cleansing of the soul. Just as ritual *catharsis* allowed the formerly polluted person to return to the community and take part in communal life without bringing *miasma* with him, so the metaphorical *catharsis* from watching tragedy gave the spectators a shared experience that bound them closer together. In other works, Aristotle locates the essence of the self in perception; by sharing perception or perceiving the same things, the spectators develop a sort of common identity. Thus, for Aristotle, watching tragedies was a beneficial activity, both for the individual and the community.

Glossary

Chorus – Since Greek tragedy grew out of the performances of lyric poetry sung by large Choruses, it is only natural that the Chorus should remain a large part of Greek tragedy. Every play's Chorus (usually fourteen men) took on an identity appropriate to the play. For example, in the *Oedipus Rex*, they are old men of Thebes; in Aeschylus' *Eumenides*, they are the dread goddesses, the Furies.

The word *chorus* in Greek means "dance," and the Chorus' main function was to sing and dance lyric odes in between dramatic episodes. These odes comment on the action of the preceding episode. The Chorus could also, however, act as a character; one Chorus member would be designated leader and speak lines of dialogue, interacting with the other characters on stage. They react as their characters should—in the *Oedipus Rex*, the Chorus, while concerned about Oedipus' personal problems, care first and foremost about the fate of the city and finding a cure for the plague.

Cithaeron – the mountain in southern Boeotia (the region in which Thebes is located) where Oedipus was to have been exposed as an infant. Cithaeron's position on the border of Theban territory allowed Laius' herdsman to encounter someone who worked for Polybus of Corinth.

Daimones – In addition to major gods and goddesses like Zeus and Apollo, the Greeks believed in divine forces, not quite gods, who could influence human life and events. They acted somewhat like guardian angels, but could also be malicious. The word "demons" comes directly from the Greek word *daimones*.

Gods and goddesses – Greek religion was polytheistic; the Greeks worshipped many gods. The most powerful god was Zeus, the sky god, who was thought to have taken power when he overthrew his father Cronus. After Zeus came the other Olympian deities, including Zeus' queen Hera, his brother Poseidon, and his children Athena, Ares, Artemis, and Apollo. There were also other gods, older deities from the reign of Cronus who remained powerful and were often irrational. Among these are the Furies, dreadful goddesses who hunt down and drive mad humans who kill blood-relatives.

The most important god for the *Oedipus Rex* is Apollo, whose oracle at Delphi gives the important prophecies to Oedipus and Creon (Laius was traveling to this oracle when he was killed). Apollo's knowledge is absolute—if Apollo says something will happen, it will happen. His prophecies in this play, however, are not warnings: He does not tell Laius not to have children, merely that his child will kill him. He does not tell Oedipus to kill his father, but that he will kill his father. When Oedipus sends Creon to find out how to end the plague, Apollo tells them to drive the murderer of Laius out of Thebes, but this is not an instruction so much as a simple answer.

Two other gods mentioned are both sons of Zeus: Hermes, divine messenger and patron of cattle-rustlers, and Dionysus, god of wine and ecstatic intoxication. In myth, Dionysus was accompanied by satyrs (crudely sexual half-gods) and enraptured nymphs called *maenads*. He was also the god of theatre, and Greek tragedies were performed at a festival in his honor.

Hybris (hubris) – Debate over the precise meaning of this word, so important for our understanding of Greek literature and Greek law, has been going on for centuries, and studies still come out offering new interpretations. In his *Rhetoric*, the great philosopher Aristotle, who lived in Athens in the century after Sophocles' death, defined *hybris* as physical or verbal assault that brings shame to the victim, but no reward to the agent other than the personal satisfaction received from inflicting disgrace on another. Aristotle associates the act of *hybris* with the state of anger. (It is important to note that *hybris* is the act of violence itself; modern readers often make the mistake of thinking of it as some kind of attitude or pride.)

In Athenian law, *hybris* was more serious than simple assault, whether the act was physical or verbal; it could be punished by death. Because someone who got away with *hybris* would have placed himself in a position of superiority, the Chorus of our play can say that "*hybris* creates a tyrant" by giving him power over other men.

Originally, the idea of *hybris* seems to have referred to cultivated plants that grew beyond their designated boundaries and, thus, had to be pruned; eventually, its metaphorical application to humans became the only meaning of the word.

Oracles – In order to understand the will of the gods, the Greeks consulted oracles. These were places holy to a specific deity (often Apollo); humans could pose questions and the god would answer through a chosen intermediary. The most important oracle in the Greek world was Apollo's temple at Delphi (also called Pytho, because legend said that it was founded when Apollo killed the previous resident, a giant snake, or *python*.). Here, Apollo answered questions through his priestess, the Pythia, who entered an ecstatic state and babbled out responses, which were in turn interpreted and delivered in verse by the priests. It was customary for kings and cities to consult the oracle of Delphi before making any big decision.

Pollution (*miasma*) – Murder and incest violate natural law as well as human law, so these crimes were seen to offend the gods. Both the agent and location of the crime were polluted by the act, as were people or places harboring the polluted individual; proper ritual cleansing (*catharsis*) was necessary to restore both person and place to an acceptable state. In the presence of pollution, sacrifices and prayers would be ignored by the gods, who were offended by the pollution. Hence, the community had to become involved— just one polluted person could destroy an entire city, which is the case in the beginning of the *Oedipus Rex*, when the presence of Laius' uncleansed murderer brings a plague upon Thebes. Apollo's oracle tells the Thebans to either kill or drive out the guilty man, which will remove the source of pollution from Thebes. Assuming that the guilty man left Thebes for voluntary exile, he could approach a temple or powerful person and ask for ritual cleansing, at which point he would not longer be considered polluted or bring pollution upon his location.

Religion – For the most part, Greek religion did not follow a moral code. The Greeks did not love their gods, but respected their power. Humans won the favor of the gods through sacrifice and offerings, whether blood sacrifice of an animal (the kind of animal would be determined by tradition and the means of the sacrificer); pouring out a liquid offering (libation) of milk, wine, or honey; placing a gift of flowers or incense by the statue of a god; or dedicating an object of value in a temple. In return for such gifts, the gods would heed one's prayers. Since crimes like homicide or incest offended the gods (see "pollution"), they threatened the effectiveness of the prayers and sacrifices of the entire community, so the entire community could become involved in punishing those crimes.

Sphinx – a monster sent by the goddess Hera against the city of Thebes. The Sphinx was part lion, part eagle, and part woman; she asked a riddle and devoured anyone who could not answer it. When Oedipus correctly answered the riddle, the Sphinx threw herself from a cliff and perished, thus ending the terror at Thebes.

Suppliant – anyone who makes a request or prayer from a position of powerlessness. In Greek culture, the suppliant was a sacred position with special rights, responsibilities, and visual symbols. Suppliants wore or carried special emblems, such as olive branches, to identify themselves. Traditionally, they knelt before the person they were supplicating and touched either his knees or chin (it was thought that the knees and chin were directly connected to a person's heart). Suppliants also took refuge at altars. It was taboo to harm a suppliant, and anyone who did so would be cursed.

Stage directions – The manuscripts of Greek tragedies do not give stage directions, so we must figure out for ourselves the entrances and exits of characters. The dialogue, however, is filled with special clues for directions, especially Greek words that one uses when pointing. Hence, we can often tell when a character would gesture.

Tyche – Chance. This force was personified by the Greeks as a fickle goddess. *Tyche* governed coincidences, simple mistakes, and luck, whether good or bad. When Oedipus declares himself a child of Chance, he does not seriously mean that this goddess is his mother, but that his life has been dominated by fortune, as he is a foundling who became a king.

Thebes – one of the major cities in Greece (one of Athens' rivals in Sophocles' time) and the scene of the action of the *Oedipus Rex*. Hera sends the monstrous Sphinx to punish Thebes; when Oedipus defeats the Sphinx, he earns the kingship, marrying the queen Jocasta, widowed by the murder of Laius. The city of Thebes played a large role in Greek mythology—the "Theban cycle" in epic rivaled the "Trojan cycle" of the Iliad and Odyssey. Many Greek tragedies are set in Thebes besides the *Oedipus*, e.g. Aeschylus' *Seven Against Thebes*, Sophocles' *Antigone*, and Euripides' *Bacchae*.

Tyrannus – *Oedipus Rex* is the Latin title of a play that was called *Oedipus Tyrannus* in Greek. The English translation is "Oedipus the King."

The Ancient Greeks had two words for "king": *basileus*, which indicated a hereditary king, and *tyrannus*, which was used for kings who had not inherited their throne, but taken it. *Tyrannus* did not have the negative connotations that "tyrant" has for us today, although to the freedom-loving men of the Athenian democracy, tyranny of any kind was as unacceptable as it is to us.

Vocabulary

antistrophe – the part of a choral ode or kommos following the strophe; metrically identical to the strophe

aulos – a wind instrument which accompanied the Chorus

catharsis – a ritual purification of pollution; used by Aristotle for the purging of strong emotions achieved while watching tragedy

Chorus – a group of characters who act as a collective; in *Oedipus*, they speak for the city

demigod – the child of a god and a mortal or nymph

epic – a long poem about legendary figures and their heroic deeds

episode – the part of a Greek drama that takes place between the odes; spoken rather than sung

epode – the part of a choral ode that follows the strophe and antistrophe

hamartia – a flaw or mistake; in Greek tragedy, one that leads to the tragic hero's downfall

hybris – an act of physical or verbal assault which brings no satisfaction other than the disgrace of another

kommos – a lyric song sung by dramatic characters and the Chorus together, usually at a point of heightened emotion

lyric – poetry meant to be sung

meter – the rhythmic division of lines in poetry

miasma – pollution (see glossary)

ode – a sung piece between episodes consisting of matched lyric stanzas; also called a *stasimon*

oracle – a holy place where gods pronounced the future or divine will to mortals or those pronouncements

orchestra – the round circle in front of the stage where the Chorus danced

Paean – a ritual hymn of thanks given to Apollo for a cure from sickness or injury, as well as another name for Apollo in his capacity as healer

parodos – the first entrance of the Chorus

peripeteia – the reversal of fortune

prologue – the part of the tragedy before the Chorus' entrance

stasimon – the Greek term for ode; takes place between dramatic episodes, allowing the Chorus to reflect on the action and dialogue that has preceded

strophe – the first part of a choral ode or kommos

tragedy – a type of dramatic genre, loftier and more serious than comedy, often with a sad ending

tyche – the Greek word for "chance," personified as a goddess

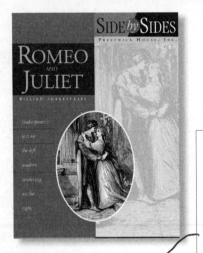

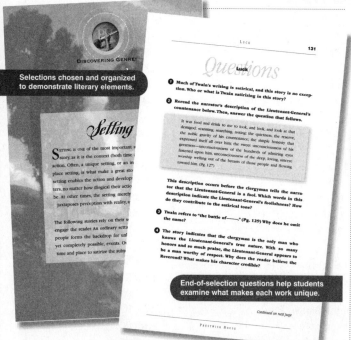

Insightful and Reader-Friendly, Yet Affordable

Prestwick House Literary Touchstone Classic Editions–
The Editions By Which All Others May Be Judged

Every *Prestwick House Literary Touchstone Classic* is enhanced with Reading Pointers for Sharper Insight to improve comprehension and provide insights that will help students recognize key themes, symbols, and plot complexities. In addition, each title includes a Glossary of the more difficult words and concepts.

For the Shakespeare titles, along with the Reading Pointers and Glossary, we include margin notes and various strategies to understanding the language of Shakespeare.

New titles are constantly being added; call or visit our website for current listing.

Special Introductory Educator's Discount – At Least 50% Off

		Retail Price	Intro. Discount
X200102	Red Badge of Courage, The	~~$3.99~~	$1.99
X200163	Romeo and Juliet	~~$3.99~~	$1.99
X200074	Heart of Darkness	~~$3.99~~	$1.99
X200079	Narrative of the Life of Frederick Douglass	~~$3.99~~	$1.99
X200125	Macbeth	~~$3.99~~	$1.99
X200053	Adventures of Huckleberry Finn, The	~~$4.99~~	$2.49
X200081	Midsummer Night's Dream, A	~~$3.99~~	$1.99
X200179	Christmas Carol, A	~~$3.99~~	$1.99
X200150	Call of the Wild, The	~~$3.99~~	$1.99
X200190	Dr. Jekyll and Mr. Hyde	~~$3.99~~	$1.99
X200141	Awakening, The	~~$3.99~~	$1.99
X200147	Importance of Being Earnest, The	~~$3.99~~	$1.99
X200166	Ethan Frome	~~$3.99~~	$1.99
X200146	Julius Caesar	~~$3.99~~	$1.99
X200095	Othello	~~$3.99~~	$1.99
X200091	Hamlet	~~$3.99~~	$1.99
X200231	Taming of the Shrew, The	~~$3.99~~	$1.99
X200133	Metamorphosis, The	~~$3.99~~	$1.99

PRESTWICK HOUSE, INC.
"Everything for the English Classroom!"

Prestwick House, Inc. • P.O. Box 658, Clayton, DE 19938
Phone (800) 932-4593 • Fax (888) 718-9333 • www.prestwickhouse.com